Contents

Contents

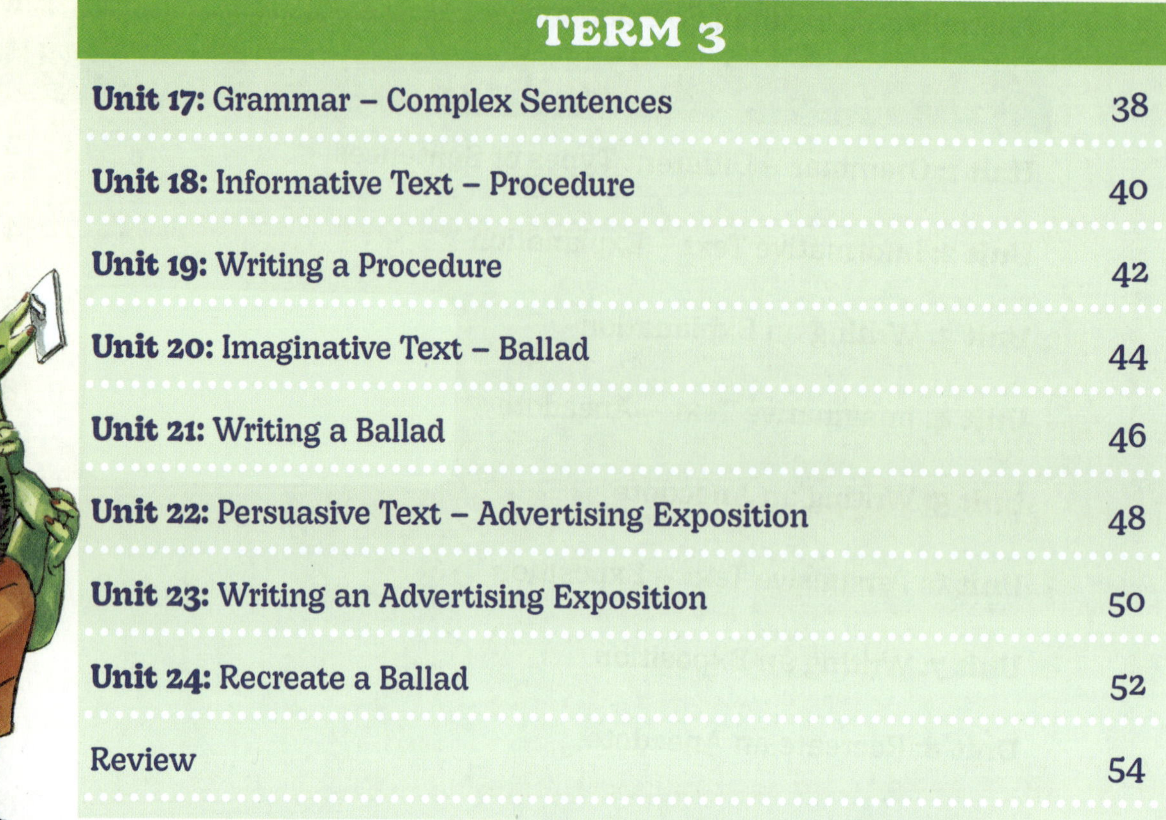

TERM 3

TERM 4

TARGETING WRITING SKILLS YR 6 © PASCAL PRESS ISBN 9781925726299

How to use this book

Targeting Writing Skills **is a comprehensive program for teaching students the fundamentals of grammar and the basic structure of the three main types of texts: Informative, Imaginative and Persuasive.**

This book is organised into four terms, each consisting of eight units of work followed by a review. The first unit of each term focuses on grammar, primarily on the structure of sentences. The following six units are organised in pairs, with each pair focusing on a different text type. The first unit of each pair introduces and explains the structure and features of the text type using an annotated example text. The second unit provides students with a stimulus appropriate to the text type and prompts to write their own text using the model as a guide.

Each term follows the same order:

- Informative texts – Units 2 &3, 10 & 11, 18 &19, 26 & 27
- Imaginative texts – Units 4 & 5, 12 & 13, 20 & 21, 28 & 29
- Persuasive texts – Units 6 & 7, 14 & 15, 22 & 23, 30 & 31

The final unit in each term provides students with additional practice in writing either an imaginative or persuasive text by innovating on an existing text to change characters, setting, text type or point of view. As these are the two main text types that students encounter in NAPLAN assessments, the additional practice helps prepare them for the tests.

A review of work that has been covered concludes the term.

While the units are organised into terms, it is not necessary to complete them sequentially. Teachers may choose units from any section of the book that suits their teaching needs. However, it is recommended that the grammar units be completed in order as each one builds upon the previous one.

The writing topics in this book were selected for their relevance to the Australian Curriculum V9, including HASS, Science, General Capabilities and Cross-curriculum Priorities so that these books can be used for lessons in writing across the curriculum.

The units are presented using a gradual release of responsibility model:

1. Information is presented and explained in a detailed model.
2. Students are supported to identify features of the model.
3. Students use the model as a guide to write a text of their own about a given stimulus.

Prior to writing their own texts, students are reminded of the required structure and parts of speech that they need to incorporate. They plan, draft and receive feedback on their text before writing a revised draft. At the conclusion, they conduct a self-evaluation to determine how well they adhered to the structure and included appropriate parts of speech.

Australian Curriculum Correlations

Code	Description	Pages
English: Language		
AC9E6LA02	understand the uses of objective and subjective language, and identify bias	4–17, 22–35, 40–53, 58–71
AC9E6LA03	explain how texts across the curriculum are typically organised into characteristic stages and phases depending on purposes, recognising how authors often adapt text structures and language features	4–17, 22–35, 40–53, 58–71
AC9E6LA04	understand that cohesion can be created by the intentional use of repetition, and the use of word associations	4–17, 22–35, 40–53, 58–71
AC9E6LA05	understand how embedded clauses can expand the variety of complex sentences to elaborate, extend and explain ideas	38–39, 56–57
AC9E6LA06	understand how ideas can be expanded and sharpened through careful choice of verbs, elaborated tenses and a range of adverb groups	3, 5, 18, 26, 27, 30–31, 33, 35, 57, 58–59, 61
AC9E6LA07	identify and explain how images, figures, tables, diagrams, maps and graphs contribute to meaning	4, 8, 12, 18, 22, 26, 30, 40, 42, 44, 48, 52, 54, 58, 62, 66, 70
AC9E6LA08	identify authors' use of vivid, emotive vocabulary, such as metaphors, similes, personification, idioms, imagery and hyperbole	8, 10, 12–15, 16, 26, 30–33, 44–45, 48–49, 52, 62–63, 66–69, 70
AC9E6LA09	understand how to use the comma for lists, to separate a dependent clause from an independent clause, and in dialogue	8–11, 16–17, 20–21, 22–23, 24, 38–39, 44, 56–57
English: Literature		
AC9E6LE01	identify responses to characters and events in literary texts, drawn from historical, social or cultural contexts, by First Nations Australians, and wide-ranging Australian and world authors	26–29, 66–71
AC9E6LE04	explain the way authors use sound and imagery to create meaning and effect in poetry	44–45, 52–53, 62–65
AC9E6LE05	create and edit literary texts that adapt plot structure, characters, settings and/or ideas from texts students have experienced, and experiment with literary devices	10–11, 16–17, 28–29, 46–47, 52–53, 64–65
English: Literacy		
AC9E6LY01	examine texts including media texts that represent ideas and events, and identify how they reflect the context in which they were created	12–13, 48–49
AC9E6LY03	analyse how text structures and language features work together to meet the purpose of a text, and engage and influence audiences	4–17, 22–35, 40–53, 58–71
AC9E6LY06	plan, create, edit and publish written and multimodal texts whose purposes may be imaginative, informative and persuasive, using paragraphs, a variety of complex sentences, expanded verb groups, tense, topic-specific and vivid vocabulary, punctuation, spelling and visual features	6–7, 10–11, 14–15, 16–17, 18–19, 24–25, 28–29, 32–33, 34–35, 36–37, 42–43, 46–47, 50–51, 52–53, 54–55, 60–61, 64–65, 68–69, 70–71, 72–73

TARGETING WRITING SKILLS YR 6 © PASCAL PRESS ISBN 9781925726299

Australian Curriculum Correlations

Code	Description	Pages
Science: Biological sciences		
AC9S6U01	investigate the physical conditions of a habitat and analyse how the growth and survival of living things is affected by changing physical conditions	30–31, 32–33, 34–35, 52–53, 70–71
Science: Physical sciences		
AC9S6U03	investigate the transfer and transformation of energy in electrical circuits, including the role of circuit components, insulators and conductors	4–7
Science: Chemical sciences		
AC9S6U04	compare reversible changes, including dissolving and changes of state, and irreversible changes, including cooking and rusting that produce new substances	40–43
HASS: History		
AC9HS6K01	significant individuals, events and ideas that led to Australia's Federation, the Constitution and democratic system of government	12, 58
AC9HS6K02	changes in Australia's political system and to Australian citizenship after Federation and throughout the 20th century that impacted First Nations Australians, migrants, women and children	14–15, 60–61, 66–67
HASS: Geography		
AC9HS6K04	the geographical diversity and location of places in the Asia region, and its location in relation to Australia	22–25
HASS: Civics and citizenship		
AC9HS6K06	the key institutions of Australia's system of government, how it is based on the Westminster system, and the key values and beliefs of Western democracies	14–15
HASS: Economics and business		
AC9HS6K08	influences on consumer choices and strategies that can be used to help make informed personal consumer and financial choices	16–17, 30–35, 48–51
HASS: Communicating		
AC9HS6S07	present descriptions and explanations, drawing ideas, findings and viewpoints from sources, and using relevant terms and conventions	6–7, 14–15, 24–25, 32–35, 42–43, 50–51, 60–61, 68–71

GRAMMAR Different types of sentences

A sentence is a group of words that makes sense on its own. It always has a verb. It usually has a subject and often has an object.

A statement is a sentence that gives information or an opinion. A statement begins with a capital letter and usually ends with a full stop.
Examples: *All objects are made up of atoms.* (information)
All objects are beautiful. (opinion)

A question is a sentence that asks for more information. A question begins with a capital letter and ends with a question mark. Questions often begin with who, what, where, when, why and how.
Example: *What is static electricity?*
Questions may begin with other words too.
Example: *Did you know that lightning is caused by static electricity?*

A command is a sentence that gives instructions or directions. A command begins with a capital letter and may end with a full stop or an exclamation mark. The first word is usually a verb, and the subject (you) is understood.
Examples: *Stay inside during the thunderstorm.*
Run!

An exclamation expresses sudden surprise, joy or fright. An exclamation begins with a capital letter and ends with an exclamation mark. Some exclamations are just one word. They may not have a verb and may not be a complete sentence.
Examples: *Hooray! That's fantastic! Well done! Stop it! Look out! Danger!*

1 **Read these sentences. Write S if the sentence is a statement, Q if it asks a question and C if the sentence gives an instruction. Write E if it is an exclamation.**

- ☐ **a** Why should you stay inside in a thunderstorm?
- ☐ **b** Put your umbrella away when you come inside.
- ☐ **c** Close the door!
- ☐ **d** Crikey!
- ☐ **e** The Bureau of Meteorology warned of a severe thunderstorm.

2 **Write some sentences about this picture. Remember to punctuate your sentences correctly.**

a (S) ______________________________________

____

b (Q) ______________________________________

____

c (C) ______________________________________

____

d (E) ______________________________________

____

TARGETING WRITING SKILLS YR 6 © PASCAL PRESS ISBN 9781925726299

GRAMMAR Verbs and verb groups

Every sentence has a verb. **Verbs consist of one or more words that tell us what is 'going on' in a sentence.**

Verb categories

Doing or action verbs: *run, hop, cut, mix, pick*
Saying or speaking verbs: *mumble, shout, whisper, groan, snigger*
Thinking verbs: *imagine, believe, wonder, consider, realise*
Feeling verbs: *like, respect, forgive, admire, embarrass*
Being verbs: *am, is, are, was, were*
Having verbs: *has, have, had*

Being and having words can be used on their own. They can also be used to form verb groups and 'help' other verbs.

Examples: *I **am waiting** for the bus.*
*I **have been waiting** for the bus for a long time.*

Verbs and verb groups

A verb can be one word.
Example: *The lightning **hit** the tree.*
A verb group is made up of two or more words.
Example: *The tree **was struck** by lightning.*

3 **Read these sentences. Circle the verbs. Write the category to which the verbs belong. Remember, a verb may consist of one or more words.**

a Forgive your enemies. ____________________
b Who is whispering behind the door? ____________________
c The car was going too fast along the road. ____________________
d Suddenly, Matt realised his mistake. ____________________
e The class will have an excursion to the zoo next week. ____________________

Verb tense

Verb tense tells when something happens — in the present (now), in the past or in the future.

4 **Read these sentences. Circle the verbs. Remember, a verb may consist of one or more words. Write N if the verb is present tense, P if it is past tense or F if it is future tense.**

☐ a I rode my bike to school.
☐ b Australia is a federation of six states.
☐ c We will keep working until the end of term.
☐ d It has been raining for more than two weeks.
☐ e They had been building the house until the rain started.

5 **Write some sentences of your own in present (N), past (P) and future (F) tense.**

a (N) ____________________
b (P) ____________________
c (F) ____________________

INFORMATIVE TEXTS Explanation

The purpose of an explanation is to explain how or why something in the world happens or how things work.

Purpose: This explanation explains static electricity.

Audience: The intended audience of this explanation is students who are learning about electricity and wish to have a better understanding of what static electricity is.

Context: Texts like this would be found in science textbooks and magazines, and online.

Explanations often include photographs or diagrams.

A title identifies the topic. It is often written as a question.

What is Static Electricity?

A general statement introduces the topic.

Static electricity is a build-up of charge on the surface of an object. It doesn't flow like current electricity.

All objects consist of atoms. Atoms consist of smaller particles: negatively charged electrons, positively charged protons and neutral neutrons. Mostly, the protons and electrons are balanced, and objects have no charge.

A series of paragraphs explains the process and the cause-and-effect relationships.

When surfaces of objects rub, electrons from one may move to the other. One becomes negatively charged and the other positively charged. Differently charged atoms attract, while atoms with a similar charge repel.

When you rub a balloon against your hair, the balloon takes electrons from your hair and becomes negatively charged. Your hair, now positively charged, tries to stick to the balloon. Conversely, each hair repels the others and sticks out wildly.

A concluding statement completes the explanation and links back to the introductory statement.

You may also have experienced static electricity if you were 'zapped' by a door handle, or even by shaking hands with a friend. Perhaps the biggest, hottest, loudest effect of static electricity you will experience is lightning. You see, static electricity surrounds us, but we don't always notice it.

Parts of Speech

Topic-related nouns, noun groups and technical language
- static electricity
- current electricity
- atoms
- smaller particles
- negatively charged electrons
- positively charged protons

Present tense action verbs
- flow
- rub
- move
- attract
- repel

Words to signal cause/effect
- when
- if

Words to signal comparison
- while
- conversely

Adverbial phrases
- on the surface of an object
- against your hair
- to the balloon

TARGETING WRITING SKILLS YR 6 © PASCAL PRESS ISBN 9781925726299

Structure of an explanation

Title
The title of an explanation identifies the topic. It is often written in the form of a question. Readers know that this explanation will explain static electricity.

1 **Circle the title of the explanation.**

Introductory statement
A general statement introduces the topic to focus the reader on what will be explained.

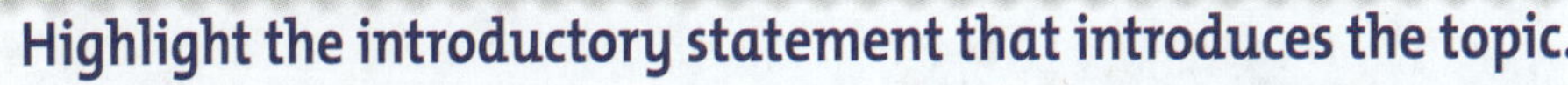

2 **Highlight the introductory statement that introduces the topic.**

A series of paragraphs
A series of paragraphs explains the process. Each paragraph has one main idea.

3 **Highlight the main idea in each paragraph. In just a few words, list the main ideas below.**

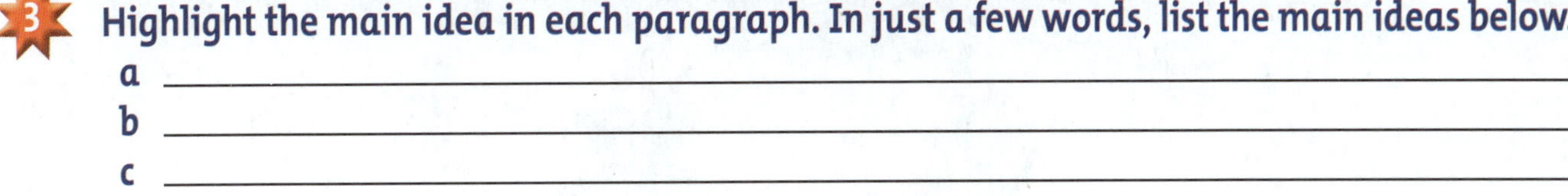

a ______________________________

b ______________________________

c ______________________________

d ______________________________

Language features of an explanation

Nouns, noun groups and technical language
Nouns are the names of things in our world such as people, places, animals and things.

In an explanation, the nouns relate to the topic. They are **topic nouns**. They may also be specialised or **technical nouns**.

Topic and technical nouns are often repeated to link the text and ensure it can be understood. For example, *electricity* and *charge* are repeated throughout the text.

4 **Circle each time the words *electricity* or *charge* appear in the text.**

A **noun group** is a group of words built around a noun to give it more meaning.

Sometimes the adjective *charged* is used to form a noun group.

Example: *negatively charged atoms*

5 **Circle the nouns groups with the adjective *charged*. List them below.**

a ______________________________

b ______________________________

c ______________________________

d ______________________________

Verbs and tense
Explanations use *being* words to explain what is and *doing* words to explain the actions. They are usually written in present tense.

6 **Read these sentences. Highlight the verb. Write B if the verb is a being verb. Write D if it is a doing verb. Remember, a verb may consist of one or more words.**

☐ a Static electricity is a build-up of charge on the surface of an object.

☐ b Mostly, the protons and electrons are balanced.

☐ c Differently charged atoms attract.

☐ d Your hair tries to stick to the balloon.

7 a Find a sentence in the text that is written in past tense. Write it here.

____

b Find a sentence in the text that is written in future tense. Write it here.

____

Use the previous information about static electricity, this diagram, and these notes to write an explanation of what causes lightning.

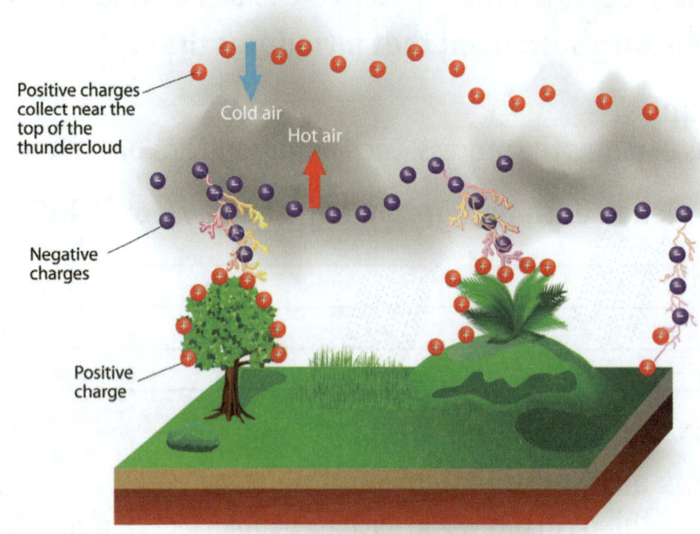

Lightning

- inside clouds – water droplets and ice particles collide
- negatively charged water droplets or ice particles collect at base of cloud
- the base of the clouds becomes negatively charged (–)
- when negatively charged clouds are close to something positively charged (+), like a tree, the ground or another cloud, the electrical charge moves, making lightning

Plan

1. Write the title for your explanation. Remember to write it as a question.

___

2. Write a general statement to introduce your explanation.

___

3. Write a few words about the main idea for each paragraph.

a ___
b ___
c ___

4. List the doing verbs that you will use to explain what happens.

___

5. In your own words, rewrite the information from the article on static electricity that you will use in your explanation.

___
___
___

 TARGETING WRITING SKILLS YR 6 © PASCAL PRESS ISBN 9781925726299

Draft

Now you are ready to write an explanation of what causes lightning.

Remember to:

- write your title as a question first
- write a general statement to introduce your topic
- explain the process in a series of paragraphs
- write a statement to conclude your explanation
- use present tense
- write in sentences with capital letters and full stops.

First draft

Write a draft of your explanation here.

Feedback

Ask your teacher, classmates or someone at home to suggest what you could do to improve your explanation.

Revised draft

Self-evaluation

I wrote ☐ the title as a question.
☐ an introductory statement.
☐ a concluding statement.
☐ in sentences with capital letters and full stops.

I used ☐ present tense verbs.

I explained ☐ the process in a series of paragraphs.

IMAGINATIVE TEXTS Anecdote

The purpose of an anecdote is to relate an incident or event in a humorous or unusual way. An anecdote is similar to a recount, but it is usually funny and imaginative in that it tends to stretch the truth a little.

Purpose: This anecdote retells a family event in a humorous way to entertain.

Audience: The intended audience is people who enjoy reading short, funny personal stories.

Context: Anecdotes like this may be found in humorous columns in magazines or may be told by characters in novels and plays. They may also be found online.

Anecdotes, if published in magazines, may include illustrations.

A heading or title introduces the anecdote.

Forbidden Fruit

An introductory paragraph sets the scene. It introduces the who, where and when.

My father bought several dwarf pear trees which he planted in the yard around the house. He watered them and fed them and watched them grow for many years. When at last one of the trees produced just one pear, he warned us that, under no circumstances, were we to pull that pear off the tree. "Whoever pulls that pear off the tree will be grounded for life," he said.

A middle explains the problem and how the characters try to solve it.

Every day, the pear grew larger, riper and more lusciously tempting. The sight of it made our mouths water — especially as we were forbidden to pull it off!

A conclusion, usually humorous, explains how the problem was solved.

However, one of his children (I won't say who), carefully reasoned that it was not forbidden to touch the pear, nor even to eat it, only that it must not be "pulled off". That child bent down the limb that bore the pear, ate the juicy fruit, and left the core hanging on the tree!

Parts of Speech

Topic-related nouns and noun groups
- trees
- yard
- pear
- limb

Hyperbole
- under no circumstances
- grounded for life
- lusciously tempting

Past tense
- bought
- planted
- watered
- grew

Thinking and saying verbs
- warned
- said
- reasoned

First-person narrator pronouns
- my
- us
- we
- our
- I

TARGETING WRITING SKILLS YR 6 © PASCAL PRESS ISBN 9781925726299

Structure of an anecdote

Heading
A heading or title introduces the anecdote.

Circle the heading of the anecdote.

Opening statements
The opening statements introduce the scene, telling who the anecdote is about and where and when it takes place.

Highlight the opening statements that introduce the scene.

Middle
The middle explains the problem and what the characters do to solve the problem.

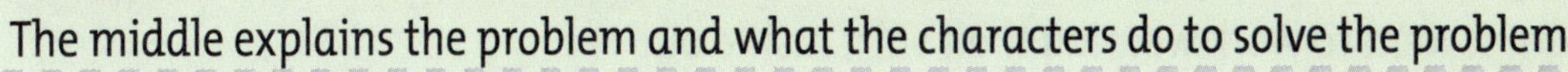

In your own words, write what the problem is.

____

____

Conclusion
A conclusion, which is usually humorous, explains how the problem is solved.

a Highlight the conclusion.
b Explain what makes this conclusion humorous.

____

____

Language features of an imaginative anecdote

First- and third-person narrators
Most of the text is told by a first-person narrator. It may be a child telling the story or an adult telling a story from their childhood. A first-person narrator uses *I, my, we, our* and *us* to refer to the children in the family.

Circle the pronouns that show the text is told by a first-person narrator.

The final paragraph is written as if by a third-person narrator, as if the writer is an onlooker and not one of the children. The narrator changed the point of view to avoid giving away the identity of the pear thief. It adds to the humour. By not revealing the thief, the narrator may be admitting to being the thief. Or, with a wink, may incriminate a sibling.

Rewrite the final paragraph as if the narrator was the culprit and admitting it.

____

____

____

Direct speech
Direct speech refers to the exact words spoken by a character. Direct speech is shown using speech marks, or inverted commas at the beginning and end of the words spoken.
Example: *"Whoever pulls that pear off the tree will be grounded for life,"* he said.
A comma, question mark or exclamation mark separates the spoken words from the unspoken words that tell who the speaker is; for example, *he said*.

Using direct speech, write the exact words that the father may have said when he saw what happened to the pear. Write what his children or the child may have said in reply.

____

____

____

TERM ONE

UNIT 5

FOCUS ON

IMAGINATIVE TEXTS Writing an imaginative anecdote

Write an anecdote about a humorous event that has occurred in your family or amongst your friends. Anecdotes are the funny stories you tell each other to get a laugh. They may be mostly true but don't have to be exactly true. You can stretch the truth a little using hyperbole or exaggeration.
Pets and younger siblings are usually good subjects for anecdotes; parents can be too.

Here are some suggestions to get you thinking, but you may choose a situation of your own.

- The day you were locked out of the house
- Your parent went to work wearing their shirt inside out
- You found your baby sister drawing on walls with your mother's lipstick
- You put a doughnut-shaped bath bomb in your brother's lunch
- Your cat got stuck in a tree
- Your friend kicked the football so far that it broke the neighbour's window
- Your sister used shaving cream instead of toothpaste

Plan

1 **In a few words explain the situation.**

2 **Who is the anecdote mainly about?**

3 **Who else is in the story?**

4 **Write an opening statement to introduce the scene.**

5 **Write notes about the events that occurred.**

6 **Write what happens at the end and explain why it is funny.**

7 **Direct speech**
What are some things that were or may have been said? Remember to use inverted commas and speaking verbs.

8 **Write parts of your story that you could exaggerate.**

9 **How will you tell your story?** ☐ first-person narrator ☐ third-person narrator

10 **Write a conclusion for your anecdote.**

TARGETING WRITING SKILLS YR 6 © PASCAL PRESS ISBN 9781925726299

Draft

Now you are ready to write a draft of your anecdote.

Remember to:

- write a heading for your anecdote first
- write an opening statement to introduce the scene
- tell the events in order
- write a conclusion for your anecdote
- use exaggeration to increase the humour of your story
- use direct speech to report what the characters say
- write in sentences with capital letters and full stops.

First draft

Write a draft of your anecdote here.

Feedback

Ask your teacher, classmates or someone at home to suggest what you could do to improve your anecdote.

Revised draft

Self-evaluation

I wrote ☐ a heading on the first line.
☐ an opening statement to introduce the scene.
☐ a conclusion.
☐ in sentences with capital letters and full stops.

I used ☐ exaggeration to increase humour.
☐ inverted commas and speaking verbs to show direct speech.

I told ☐ the events in order.

PERSUASIVE TEXTS Exposition

An exposition is also known as an argument. It is used to put forward one point of view, either for or against a particular idea. The writer's aim is to justify their point of view so that they will persuade the audience to agree with them, as in this speech by Sir Henry Parkes.

Purpose: This exposition, a speech, was to convince the people of Australia that it was time to form a federation.

Audience: The audience of this speech was the people of Australia. It was considered groundbreaking because it was the first time the common people, as opposed to politicians, had been addressed.

Context: Transcripts and extracts of speeches, such as this one, can be found in newspapers, political magazines and online.

The persuasive text may be accompanied by a photograph or illustration.

A heading introduces the topic.

The Tenterfield Oration by Sir Henry Parkes (1889, an extract)

An opening statement attracts attention and identifies the point of view (P).

The great question which we have to consider is whether the time has not now arisen for the creation on this Australian continent of an Australian government and an Australian parliament.

A series of arguments is presented in separate paragraphs. They provide evidence (E) and explain (E) reasons for holding the point of view.

To make myself as plain as possible, Australia has now a population of three and a half million, and the American people numbered only between three and four million when they formed the great Commonwealth of the United States. The numbers are about the same. Surely what the Americans have done by war, Australians can bring about in peace.

Believing, as I do, that it is essential to preserve the security and integrity of these colonies, then the whole of our forces should be amalgamated into one great Federal army.

A concluding statement reinforces the point of view by linking (L) back to the main argument.

Seeing no other means of obtaining these ends, it seems to me that the time is close at hand when we ought to set about creating this great national Government for all Australia.

Parts of Speech

Topic-related nouns and noun groups
- Australian government
- parliament
- population
- Federal army
- great national Government

Present tense
- has arisen
- are
- can bring

Modal verbs
- have to consider
- can
- should be amalgamated
- ought to set

Emotive and evaluative words
- great question
- as plain as possible
- surely
- essential

TARGETING WRITING SKILLS YR 6 © PASCAL PRESS ISBN 9781925726299

Structure of an exposition

PEEL

An exposition is often written using what is known as the PEEL structure.

(P) The heading and opening statements of an exposition often introduce the topic and point of view. Because this exposition is the record of a famous speech which was made in the past, the heading tells us who made the speech and where it was delivered.

1 Circle the heading of the exposition.

Opening statement

The opening statement attracts attention and identifies the point of view. Because this speech was written a long time ago, the ideas are expressed a little differently from what you may be used to. However, the point of view is still very clear.

2 Underline the statement that introduces the point of view.

3 Write the point of view in your own words.

____

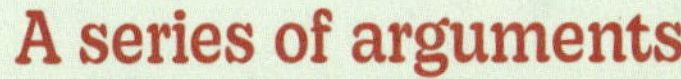

A series of arguments

A series of arguments provides evidence and explains reasons for the writer's point of view. Each argument is written in a separate paragraph.

(E) One clause or sentence in each paragraph provides the evidence or reasons for the point of view.

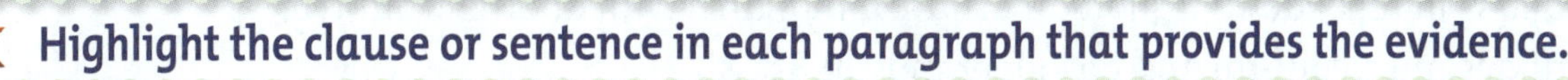

4 Highlight the clause or sentence in each paragraph that provides the evidence.

(E) Other clauses and sentences explain why the evidence is important.

5 Underline clauses and sentences that explain why the evidence is important.

(L) Each argument links back to the initial statement expressing the writer's point of view. You will see this by the repetition of words referring to Australia, government, federal or national.

6 Circle each time words are used to refer to Australia united as one nation.

The final statement also links back to the initial statement by restating and reinforcing the writer's position.

7 Highlight the final statement that reinforces the writer's position.

Language features of an exposition

Thinking and feeling words and phrases

In this speech, the writer uses words and phrases to emphasise that this is his point of view.

8 Write the words and phrases that show the writer is expressing his own opinion.

____

____

Emotive and evaluative words

In an exposition, emotive and evaluative words are used to make the reader feel the same way about the topic as the writer does.

9 a Use a red pencil to circle all the emotive and evaluative words in the text.

b Write them here.

____

____

10 In your own words, write the main point of the exposition.

____

____

Writing an exposition

Should Australia be a Republic?

In 1999 a referendum was held to establish Australia as a republic with a President, replacing the British Monarch as head of state. The people voted 'no', but the discussion about whether Australia should be a republic continues.

Read these arguments for and against Australia becoming a republic. Decide whether you are in favour of maintaining the monarchy or establishing a republic. Write an exposition that you could deliver as a speech to convince others to agree with you.

Arguments for a republic

- The position of the monarch is symbolic. It has no real power.
- An Australian citizen should be Australia's head of state.
- Australia is independent. It shouldn't share a monarch with another country.
- Australia is multicultural and no longer mostly British.
- Inherited privilege does not belong in Australia's way of life.

Arguments for keeping the reigning monarch as Head of State

- A monarch has always been Australia's head of state.
- The monarchy keeps us in the British Commonwealth. This means we can still compete in the Commonwealth Games.
- Immigrants enjoy the stability of life under the monarchy.
- A president won't make any real difference.

Plan

1 **What is your point of view? Write it as a heading.**

____

2 **Write an opening statement to attract attention and identify your point of view.**

____

____

3 **In the notes, tick ✓ two arguments you consider most important to your point of view.**

4 **Write reasons you consider those arguments to be important.**

____

____

5 **List emotive words you could use to emphasise your arguments.**

____

6 **Add other opinions you may have that support your argument.**

____

____

Draft

Now you are ready to write a draft of your exposition.
Remember to:

- write the title to introduce the topic
- (P) write an opening statement to attract attention and identify your opinion
- (E) write short paragraphs to provide evidence for your opinion
- (E) write statements to explain why the evidence is important
- (L) restate your opinion and link your closing statement back to your opening statement
- use emotive words to influence the opinions of readers
- use capital letters at the beginning of sentences and full stops at the end.

First draft

Write a draft of your exposition here.

Feedback

Ask your teacher, classmates or someone at home to suggest what you could do to improve your exposition.

Revised draft

Self-evaluation

I wrote ☐ a title to identify the topic.
(P) ☐ an opening statement to identify my opinion.
(E) ☐ short paragraphs giving evidence to support my opinion.
(E) ☐ statements explaining why my evidence was important.
(L) I restated ☐ my opinion and linked my closing statement back to my opening statement.

I used ☐ emotive words.
☐ capital letters and full stops correctly.

RECREATING TEXTS Anecdote

The purpose of an anecdote is to relate an incident or event in a humorous or unusual way. An anecdote is similar to a recount, but it is usually funny and imaginative in that it tends to stretch the truth a little.

Purpose: This anecdote tells a story about a baker in a humorous way to entertain.

Audience: The intended audience is people who enjoy reading short, funny personal stories.

Context: Anecdotes like this may be found in humorous columns in magazines or may be told by characters in novels and plays. They may also be found online.

Holey Doughnuts

There once was a baker who was famous for making the best doughnuts in the land. People queued for hours to buy them. The baker was happy as she was making a lot of money from her mouth-watering doughnuts.

Life was sweet until one day, when the baker was thinking about the hole in the doughnut, she had an idea. She thought that she could make more money, more quickly, by making the holes bigger. "More hole = less dough = more dough!" she thought.

She immediately put her idea into action. The new doughnuts with the bigger holes were even more popular, and the baker's sales skyrocketed.

However, after a while, she realised that she wasn't making as much money as she had before. She ordered an investigation. Sadly, she discovered that she had to use more dough, not less, to go around the larger holes. So, more hole = more dough = less dough!

Imagine you are a customer at the doughnut bakery. Write an anecdote about a humorous event or discussion that occurs when you are waiting in line or purchasing your doughnuts. It may involve you or others in the queue.

Suggestions:

You queue for hours, and the doughnuts are sold by the time you get to the counter.

You see someone drop their doughnut on the ground and a dog steals it.

What situation will you write about?

____

What will make your story humorous?

____

What words may be spoken (direct speech) by the characters in your story?

____

TARGETING WRITING SKILLS YR 6 © PASCAL PRESS ISBN 9781925726299

Write an anecdote about waiting in a queue to buy doughnuts

Use your notes to write an anecdote about a humorous event that occurred in the doughnut queue. While this will be an imaginary event, you may base it on an incident you have experienced or seen. Think of what might happen in a queue, then exaggerate it to make it funny.

Remember to:

- write a heading for your anecdote first
- write an opening statement to introduce the scene
- tell the events in order
- write a conclusion for your anecdote
- use exaggeration to increase the humour of your story
- use direct speech to report what the characters say
- write in sentences with capital letters and full stops.

First draft

Write a draft of your anecdote here.

Feedback

Ask your teacher, classmates or someone at home to suggest what you could do to improve your anecdote.

Revised draft

Self-evaluation

I wrote ☐ a heading on the first line.
☐ an opening statement to introduce the scene.
☐ a conclusion.
☐ in sentences with capital letters and full stops.

I used ☐ exaggeration to increase humour.
☐ inverted commas and speaking verbs to show direct speech.

I told ☐ the events in order.

TERM 1

REVIEW

DIFFERENT TYPES OF SENTENCES

A **statement** is a sentence that gives information or an opinion.

A **question** is a sentence that asks for more information.

A **command** is a sentence that gives instructions or directions. It usually begins with a verb.

An **exclamation** expresses sudden surprise, joy or fright. It may or may not be a sentence.

1 Read the statements then rewrite them as a question (Q), command (C) and exclamation (E). Remember to use the correct punctuation.

When you rub a balloon against your hair, your hair tries to stick to it.

a (Q) ______________________________

b (C) ______________________________

c (E) ______________________________

2 The children were forbidden to pick the only pear on the tree.

a (Q) ______________________________

b (C) ______________________________

c (E) ______________________________

VERBS AND VERB GROUPS

Verbs tell us what is 'going on' in a sentence. They may consist of one or more words.

Categories of verbs are *doing, saying, thinking, feeling, being* or *having*.

Verb tense tells when something happens in the present, past or future.

3 Read these sentences. Circle the verbs.

Write **N** if the verb is present tense, **P** if it is past tense or **F** if it is future tense.

Write the category to which the verbs belong.

☐ **a** I know all about static electricity. ____________________

☐ **b** Henry Parkes delivered the Tenterfield Oration in 1889. ____________________

☐ **c** A huge crowd queued at the doughnut bakery. ____________________

☐ **d** Crikey! It will be a very wet summer. ____________________

INFORMATIVE TEXT – Explanation

An explanation explains how or why something in the world happens or how things work.

4 Use these notes and the explanation of static electricity on page 4 to explain why you sometimes get zapped by a metal doorhandle after walking across a carpeted floor when you are wearing shoes with rubber or plastic soles.

- doorhandle – no charge
- carpet – no charge
- shoes rub against carpet – pick up electrons – you become negatively charged
- if the doorhandle is positively charged when you touch it – zap!

____

____

____

____

TARGETING WRITING SKILLS YR 6 © PASCAL PRESS ISBN 9781925726299

IMAGINATIVE TEXT – Anecdote

The purpose of an anecdote is to relate an incident or event in a humorous or unusual way. An anecdote is similar to a recount, but it is usually funny and imaginative in that it tends to stretch the truth a little.

5 Write an anecdote about a humorous event that has occurred in your family, amongst your friends or at school. Choose a different event from the one you wrote about on pages 10 and 11. Make some notes first.

a What is the situation? ______________________

b Who is the anecdote about? ______________________

c Who else is in the story? ______________________

d What happens at the end? ______________________

6 Write your anecdote in the first person if it's about you, or in the third person if it's about someone else.

____

____

____

____

____

PERSUASIVE TEXT – Exposition

The purpose of an exposition is to express opinions and argue a case either for or against a topic in order to persuade the audience to agree with them.

7 Choose one of these topics or one of your own and write an exposition to convince readers of your point of view.

- The school day should be shorter (or longer)
- Students should be paid for attending school
- The voting age should be reduced to 10 years
- Children should choose whether to attend school or not
- Everyone should play a sport

Remember to:

- write a heading to introduce your topic
- write an opening statement to identify your point of view
- explain your point of view with evidence
- use emotive language.

____

____

____

____

____

____

____

GRAMMAR Compound sentences

A **clause** is a group of words with a subject and a verb. Sentences are constructed from clauses.
A **sentence** is a group of words that makes sense on its own. It always has a verb. It usually has a subject and often has an object.
A simple sentence has one independent, or main, clause and one verb.
Example: *Lightning is an effect of static electricity.*

A compound sentence has two independent clauses joined by a conjunction such as for, and, nor, but, or, yet, so.

We can remember these conjunctions with the mnemonic, or memory aid, FANBOYS.
A comma is always written before the conjunction joining the two clauses.
Example: *The new doughnuts were even more popular, and the baker's sales skyrocketed.*
We can underline each of the independent clauses and circle the conjunction like this:
The new doughnuts were even more popular, (and) the baker's sales skyrocketed.

1 Use different colours to underline the independent clauses in these sentences. Circle the conjunction.

- a Alex likes to read science fiction stories, but she doesn't like fantasy.
- b The baker sold a lot of doughnuts, yet she made very little profit.
- c The boy was upset, for someone had stolen his tablet.
- d The people voted in a referendum, and they decided to remain a monarchy.

Nor is used to join two negative clauses. The subject and verb are reversed in the clause following *nor*, and the verb is no longer negative.
Example: *The children weren't allowed to pick the pear, nor were they allowed to eat it.*
The two simple sentences that were joined with *nor* were:
The children weren't allowed to pick the pear. They weren't allowed to eat it.

2 Rewrite these two simple sentences as one compound sentence using *nor*. Remember to reverse the subject and verb in the clause following *nor*, and put a comma before *nor*.

- a The children weren't allowed to go to the beach. They couldn't go to the movies.

  ____

- b Static electricity isn't usually dangerous. It won't hurt you.

  ____

- c Doughnuts are not expensive. They are not healthy food.

  ____

3 Write the correct FANBOYS conjunction to join these clauses.

- a The baker made the holes bigger, __________ she could make more money.
- b The people didn't want a president, __________ did they want to change the constitution.
- c The children caught the bus to school, __________ the car was in the workshop.
- d The farmer grew a pear tree, __________ it didn't bear much fruit.
- e I chose to go on the rollercoaster, __________ I also chose the haunted house.
- f The artist ordered ten doughnuts, __________ he didn't have enough money for even one.
- g Australia could become a republic, __________ it could stay a monarchy.

TARGETING WRITING SKILLS YR 6 © PASCAL PRESS ISBN 9781925726299

GRAMMAR Sentence fragments

If a group of words does not make sense on its own, it is not a sentence. It is a **sentence fragment.**

4 **Read these groups of words. Circle the verbs, if any, in each group. Remember, a verb may consist of one or more words.**

Write **S** if the group is a **sentence** or **F** if the group is a **fragment**. In each sentence you find, add the capital letter and full stop.

Example:

[S] Max (was surprised) by the tiny green alien.

- [ ] **a** doughnuts are delicious, but they are not good for you
- [ ] **b** Tenterfield Oration 1889
- [ ] **c** north of Australia
- [ ] **d** free-range eggs
- [ ] **e** hens can go outside during the day
- [ ] **f** fishing is a popular sport, and fish is a popular food

We often write sentence fragments when taking notes about a topic. We write the most important, or key, words that carry the information and leave out the less important words. The important words are often topic words.

5 **Read this information about adaptation. Underline the key words.**

An adaptation is anything that helps an organism survive in its environment. The environment in which an organism usually lives is called its habitat. The white fur of a polar bear is an adaptation to its environment, the icy Arctic. Polar bears have black skin underneath their fur, just like the brown bears they are descended from. White fur helps camouflage polar bears while they are hunting.

Now we can use those important words to write our notes as sentence fragments.

For example:

adaptation – helps organisms survive – habitat

polar bear – white fur – adaptation – camouflage – black skin under fur

We then use those sentence fragments to make new sentences when we write about the topic in our own words. We have to make sure not to copy the original text exactly.

Example:

Animals adapt so they can survive in the habitat in which they live.

6 **Use the sentence fragments above to write two or three sentences about the polar bear. Do not copy the original text exactly. Write it in your own words.**

____

____

____

INFORMATIVE TEXTS Sociological report

A sociological report provides information about people, countries and cultures.

Purpose: This sociological report presents information about the country, Papua New Guinea.

Audience: The intended audience of this information report is geography students and others who are interested in learning about the people, history and culture of Papua New Guinea.

Context: Texts like this would be found in atlases, encyclopedias and online.

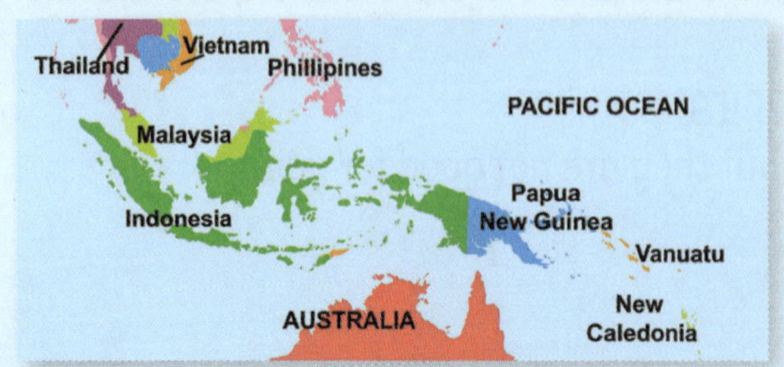

Sociological reports are usually accompanied by maps and photographs.

A general statement of topic → Country: PAPUA NEW GUINEA

Subheadings → Location: Oceania, eastern half of the island of New Guinea and offshore islands, north of Australia

Subheadings → Climate: tropical

Series of facts → Population: approx. 9 million

Series of facts → Capital: Port Moresby

Series of facts → Language: English, Hiri Motu, PNG Sign Language, Tok Pisin and 850 Indigenous languages

Currency: Kina (PGK)

Sentence fragments → Environment: mostly mountainous, covered with tropical rainforest

The history is written in sentences and in time sequence. → Trade: minerals, such as gold, oil and copper, palm oil, coffee, cocoa and coconut oil

The history is written in sentences and in time sequence. → History: The first people to live in Papua New Guinea arrived about 45,000 years ago. Until the 1800s, people lived in traditional communities. Many still do. From 1884 until 1975, Papua New Guinea was ruled by three external powers. Germany ruled the northern half of the country, called Guinea, while Britain ruled the southern part, called Papua. During World War I, Australia took over its administration.

Conclusion → The two territories combined after World War II. In 1975, they became an independent country, called Papua New Guinea.

Parts of Speech

Topic-related nouns and noun groups
- offshore islands
- tropical rainforest
- traditional communities
- administration

Third person
- the first people
- Papua New Guinea
- the two territories

Past tense
- arrived
- lived
- was ruled
- took over

Time connectives
- the first people
- about 45,000 years ago
- until the 1800s
- still
- while
- during
- after

Abbreviations
- PNG
- PGK

TARGETING WRITING SKILLS YR 6 © PASCAL PRESS ISBN 9781925726299

Structure of a sociological report

Topic

A general statement identifies the topic. In this case, it is the country about which the report is written.

Circle the general statement which introduces the sociological report.

Subheadings

Subheadings are used to organise the information.

Highlight the subheadings.

A series of facts

Each subheading is expanded with relevant facts. They are usually listed in sentence fragments or in short, simple sentences.

Write the subheading that is followed by information written in sentences.

____

Conclusion

A final sentence concludes the report.

Circle the final statement that concludes the report.

Language features of a sociological report

Sentence fragments

Information in a sociological report is often presented in sentence fragments. Sentence fragments allow more information to be shared in fewer words.

Rewrite information relating to the following subheadings in sentences.

a Climate ____

b Population ____

c Environment ____

The history of Papua New Guinea is written in sentences. It could be written as sentence fragments with times as the subheadings.
Example: *45,000 years ago* *first people arrived*

Rewrite the history of Papua New Guinea in sentence fragments using times as the subheadings.

____

____

____

Commas

Commas are used to separate three or more items in a list. The last two items are separated by *and*. A comma is not used.
Examples: *gold, oil, copper, palm oil, coffee, cocoa and coconut oil*

Write the countries that are near neighbours of Papua New Guinea in a list.

____

Abbreviations

An abbreviation is a short way of writing a word or phrase. It is often written in capitals. Full stops are not used.
Example: *AU (for Australia)*

Circle abbreviations in the report. Write them and their longer form here.

____

INFORMATIVE TEXTS Writing a sociological report

Write a sociological report about one of Australia's closest neighbours. Choose from these: New Zealand, Timor-Leste, Fiji, the Solomon Islands, New Caledonia, Indonesia, Singapore or Vanuatu.

Research the information in books, atlases or online.

Write in sentence fragments.

Country: ____________________

Location: ____________________

Climate: ____________________

Population: ____________________

Capital: ____________________

Language: ____________________

Currency: ____________________

Environment: ____________________

Trade: ____________________

Plan

1 **Make notes about the country's history. Write dates and events. Number the events in order.**

You will use this information to write a report on the country's history.

Date: __________ Event: ____________________

Date: __________ Event: ____________________

Date: __________ Event: ____________________

Date: __________ Event: ____________________

Date: __________ Event: ____________________

Date: __________ Event: ____________________

TARGETING WRITING SKILLS YR 6 © PASCAL PRESS ISBN 9781925726299

Draft

Now you are ready to write the history section of your sociological report.

Remember to:

- write a title that identifies the country
- write the subheading 'History'
- write the historical events in time sequence
- write a conclusion to the history
- write in sentences with capital letters and full stops.

First draft

Write a draft of the history section of your sociological report here.

Feedback

Ask your teacher, classmates or someone at home to suggest what you could do to improve the history section of your sociological report.

Revised draft

Self-evaluation

I wrote ☐ a title to identify the country.
☐ the subheading 'History'.
☐ the historical events in time sequence.
☐ a conclusion to the history.
☐ in my own words.
☐ in sentences with capital letters and full stops.

IMAGINATIVE TEXTS Science fiction narrative

A narrative is often referred to as a 'story'. Narratives are usually fictitious or made up. They are written to entertain or amuse the reader.

Purpose: This narrative entertains with a science fiction story.

Audience: The intended audience of this narrative is children who enjoy reading science fiction stories.

Context: This text is an episode from a longer story. Science fiction stories might be found as novels or stories in magazines.

A narrative may be accompanied by an illustration to aid meaning.

A title introduces and hints at the story.

A Moment of Accidental Stupidity

The orientation sets the scene by introducing the time, place and characters.

It was spur-of-the-moment stupidity, an accident. One minute Oz was standing on the side of the road. The next minute he was huddling behind a silver crate in a spaceship.

There is a complication or problem that affects the setting or characters.

Stamped on the crate was a picture of a constellation. It had an arrow pointing to one star. This struck Oz as an ingenious way to write an address. He just wished he knew where, exactly, that address was.

Flashbacks may be used to add tension and provide clues to the story events.

Just before the moment of accidental stupidity, Oz had been standing behind a tree when a noise like a thousand five-year-olds having lollipops plucked from their fat, little lips sounded. The dusty verge at the side of the road puffed up in a willy-willy and sailed up the road despite there being no wind. The neighbour's goat bleated a warning and galloped away, dragging its chinking chain. In the tall grass in front of Oz appeared a gigantic silver ball with an open hatch. A small hovering robot zipped out of the hatch, up over the tree where Oz stood and off across the paddock.

Episodes often conclude at an exciting point to encourage the reader to continue reading.

Parts of Speech

Topic-related nouns and noun groups
- spaceship
- constellation
- hovering robot

Adjectives
- silver
- dusty
- chinking

Similes
- like a thousand five-year-olds having lollipops plucked from their fat, little lips

Simple past tense
- was
- had
- wished
- zipped

Past continuous tense
- was standing
- was huddling

Time connectives
- one minute
- next minute
- just before
- when

Source: Extract from *Intergalactic Deliveries Inc* Bren MacDibble, Blake Education.

TARGETING WRITING SKILLS YR 6 © PASCAL PRESS ISBN 9781925726299

Structure of a science fiction narrative

Title
A title introduces and hints at the story.

1 **Circle the title of the science fiction narrative.**

Orientation
The orientation sets the scene by introducing the time, place and characters.

2
a Highlight the orientation.
b Circle the words that tell where the story takes place and the name of the character.
c Underline the words that tell you this is a science fiction story.

Complication or problem
In this story, the complication is identified immediately.

3 **In your own words, explain the problem.**

___

Flashback
A flashback goes back in time from an event already described. It may add tension or provide clues to other story events.

4
a Draw an asterisk * to show where the flashback begins.
b Write the words that tell you this is a flashback. ___

Conclusion
Episodes often conclude at an exciting point to encourage the reader to continue reading. They leave the reader wanting to know more.

5 **Write questions that you, or Oz, might ask about what has just happened. Remember to use capital letters and question marks.**
a ___
b ___
c ___

Language features of a science fiction narrative

Nouns and noun groups
Nouns and noun groups used in a science fiction narrative help to identify and describe the setting.

6 **List three things in the story that would occur only in a science fiction story.**
a ___
b ___
c ___

Past tense verbs
The story is told using past tense about events that have already happened.
Simple past tense is used to tell something that happened.
Examples: *wished, puffed up, zipped*
Past continuous tense is used to tell something that continued to happen.
Examples: *was standing, was huddling*

7 **Rewrite these sentences to change the tense of the bold verbs from simple past tense to past continuous tense.**
a Oz **watched** a robot zip across the paddock.

___

b The neighbour's goat **bleated** a warning and **galloped** away.

___

UNIT 13 FOCUS ON

IMAGINATIVE TEXTS Writing a science fiction narrative

Write your own science fiction story about an encounter between a human and an alien.
Things to consider:

Characters – Include at least one human and one alien or robot.

Setting – Decide where and when the story takes place, for example, on Earth, in space or in a spaceship.

Events – Describe how the human and alien encounter and react to each other.

Problem – Explain the problem.

Flashback – Begin part way into the story when the problem occurs, then flashback to the situation that preceded it.

Plan

1 **a** Draw a picture to illustrate the main event or problem that your characters encounter.
b Label the illustration with notes about who the characters are and what happened.

2 **List the characters' names and describe something about them.**
a ______________________________
b ______________________________

3 **Setting: Where and when does the story take place?**
Where: ______________________________
When: ______________________________

4 **How and why do the characters meet?**
____

5 **What is the problem?**
____

6 **How will you conclude the story so that readers want to continue reading?**
____
____

7 **Write a flashback to explain what the characters were doing before they met.**
____
____

TARGETING WRITING SKILLS YR 6 © PASCAL PRESS ISBN 9781925726299

Draft

Now you are ready to write a draft of your science fiction narrative.
Remember to:

- give your narrative a title
- write an orientation that sets the scene by introducing the time, place and characters
- write a series of events that occur in your story
- explain the problem
- include a flashback
- conclude your story in a way that encourages readers to continue reading
- write in sentences with capital letters and full stops.

First draft

Write a draft of your science fiction narrative here.

Feedback

Ask your teacher, classmates or someone at home to suggest what you could do to improve your science fiction narrative.

Revised draft

Self-evaluation

I wrote ☐ a title for my story.
☐ an orientation to set the scene.
☐ a series of events, including the problem.
☐ in sentences with capital letters and full stops.

I included ☐ a flashback.
I concluded ☐ my story encouraging readers to continue.

PERSUASIVE TEXTS Discussion

The purpose of a discussion is to present different points of view about an issue. It allows the reader to think about different points of view before making an informed decision.

Purpose: This discussion presents different points of view about fish farming.

Audience: The intended audience of this discussion is people who are considering the benefits and disadvantages of farming fish.

Context: Texts like this can be found in newspapers, magazines and online.

A title identifies the topic or issue. It may be in the form of a question.

A discussion may be accompanied by a photograph or illustration.

Should Fish be Farmed?

An opening statement introduces the topic and provides background information (P).

Since overfishing of our oceans has caused a decline in the numbers of fish, fish farming has become more important.

A series of paragraphs gives arguments (E) and supporting evidence (E) in favour of the topic.

Fish farms produce fish much quicker than they reproduce in the wild. Currently, about one in four fish eaten by humans has been farmed. The World Bank estimates it will increase to two-thirds by 2030. China already gets about 80% of its fish from fish farms.

Fish farms help support poorer communities by employing more people and providing a cheap source of food.

A series of paragraphs gives arguments (E) and supporting evidence (E) against the topic.

However, farmed fish eat food made from other fish. This also leads to overfishing.

Fish farms pollute by increasing algae in oceans, which reduces the amount of oxygen available for other creatures.

Keeping large numbers of animals in confined spaces can lead to disease. Antibiotics and pesticides used to combat disease can harm marine and human health. If diseased fish escape, they can infect others in the wild.

A conclusion sums up the discussion and gives a recommendation. It links (L) back to the opening statements.

Fish farming helps feed the world. However, fish farms must be managed efficiently.

Parts of Speech

Topic-related nouns and noun groups
- overfishing
- oceans
- fish
- fish farming
- fish farms

Present tense
- produce
- gets
- help support
- eat
- leads

Evaluative language
- more important
- quicker
- overfishing
- pollute
- harm
- must

Connectives
- since
- currently
- however
- also

TARGETING WRITING SKILLS YR 6 © PASCAL PRESS ISBN 9781925726299

Structure of a discussion

A discussion presents different points of view about an issue. It allows the reader to think about different points of view before making an informed decision. It may be written using what is known as the PEEL structure.

Title

The title identifies the topic or issue to be discussed. Each main word of the title is capitalised. It may take the form of a question.

1 Circle the title.

Opening statement

The opening statement introduces the topic and provides background information (P).

2 Highlight the introductory statement.

Arguments

A series of paragraphs presents arguments for and against the topic by providing evidence (E) and explanations (E).

3
- **a** Underline the arguments **for** fish farming with a green pencil.
- **b** Underline the arguments **against** fish farming with a red pencil.
- **c** Write notes as sentence fragments about each of the arguments for fish farming.

____

____

- **d** Write notes as sentence fragments about each of the arguments against fish farming.

____

____

Conclusion

The conclusion sums up the discussion, gives a recommendation and links back (L) to the opening statement.

4
- **a** Highlight the conclusion.
- **b** Write the author's recommendation for fish farming.

____

Language features of a discussion

Evaluative language

A discussion may present both points of view in a balanced way, without emphasising the benefits of one point of view and discrediting the opposite point of view.

5
- **a** Circle the evaluative words that are used to support each point of view.
- **b** Write the words here.

____

Verb tense

Discussions are often written in **present tense** to show what is happening now.
Example: *Fish farms* ***produce*** *fish much more quickly than fish can reproduce in the wild.*
Sometimes a writer uses present perfect tense to show that something was started in the past and is still continuing now.
Example: *Overfishing* ***has caused*** *a decline in the numbers of fish.*

6
- **a** There are three examples of present perfect tense in the text. Highlight the present perfect tense verb groups.
- **b** Write one of the examples here.

____

Writing a discussion

Use the information from the discussion of fish farming on page 30 and these notes to write a discussion that supports fish farming but favours freshwater farms.

Marine or Freshwater Fish Farms?

- most farmed marine fish are carnivorous – need other fish or animal protein to grow that could be used to feed people
- most farmed freshwater fish are herbivorous or omnivorous – don't need large amounts of animal protein – eat mainly natural plankton or inexpensive by-products of crops like rice
- marine environment is harsh with tides and storms – makes fish farming in ocean difficult, risky, more expensive
- cheap and easy to grow freshwater fish in inland ponds
- especially in Asia – provides jobs and income for families and small businesses
- provides a cheap form of food for poorer communities

Plan

1. Write notes from the discussion on page 30 that you will use in your discussion.

2. Write a title for your discussion.

3. Write an opening statement to introduce the topic and provide background information.

4. Highlight the words in the notes that you consider most important for the arguments. Use a different colour for each side of the argument.

5. While the notes support the idea of fish farming, they tend to favour of one type of fish farming over the other. Which is the preferred type of fish farming?

6. List the reasons that type of fish farming is preferred.

7. List disadvantages of the other form of fish farming.

8. Write a conclusion and a recommendation.

 TARGETING WRITING SKILLS YR 6 © PASCAL PRESS ISBN 9781925726299

Draft

Now you are ready to write a draft of your discussion.
Remember to:

- write a title as a question to identify the topic
- write an opening statement to introduce the topic and provide background information
- write a series of paragraphs to present arguments with evidence in favour of the topic
- write a series of paragraphs to present arguments with evidence against the topic
- write a conclusion and a recommendation
- use evaluative language to support both points of view
- write in present tense
- write in sentences with capital letters and full stops.

First draft

Write a draft of your discussion here.

Feedback

Ask your teacher, classmates or someone at home to suggest what you could do to improve your discussion.

Revised draft

Self-evaluation

I wrote
- ☐ a title as a question.
- ☐ an opening statement.
- ☐ a series of paragraphs in favour of the topic.
- ☐ a series of paragraphs against the topic.
- ☐ a conclusion and a recommendation.
- ☐ in present tense.

I used
- ☐ evaluative language to support both points of view.
- ☐ capital letters and full stops correctly in sentences.

FOCUS ON RECREATING TEXTS Persuasive text – Discussion

The purpose of a discussion is to present different points of view about an issue. It allows the reader to think about different points of view before making an informed decision.

Purpose: This discussion presents different points of view about which eggs to buy, cage eggs or free-range eggs.

Audience: The intended audience of this discussion is people who wish to make an informed choice about products they use.

Context: Discussions like this may be reported in local newspapers or in news reports on radio or television.

Eggs – Free Range or Cage?

Eggs are a popular food in Australia, with over 17 million eggs being consumed each day. When people are choosing which eggs to buy, free range or cage, they may consider things like cost, nutritional value and how the eggs have been produced, that is, how the hens have been treated.

Use the following notes to write a discussion comparing free-range and cage eggs and make a recommendation.

- cage eggs – cheaper, more affordable – 40% of eggs sold in Australian supermarkets
- without cage eggs – not enough to meet demand
- cage eggs – hens housed in large climate-controlled sheds – protected from weather and predators – rarely get sick, live longer – efficient, low cost – automated feeding, watering, ventilation, climate control, lighting, manure and egg collection – lower carbon footprint
- free range – more expensive – 47% of eggs sold
- free range – hens access outdoors when they choose during day, housed in sheds at night – can interact socially with other hens – can practise natural behaviours like nesting, foraging, perching, dust bathing – stronger bones because active – more exposed to predators and disease, a greater need for antibiotics – opportunity for fighting and pecking
- cage and free range – pretty much equal nutritionally – both mostly fed a grain-based diet

Plan

1 In the text, highlight the arguments you consider most important.

2 Write a title as a question for your discussion.

___

3 Write an opening statement to introduce the topic and provide background information.

___

4 Write a conclusion and a recommendation.

___

TARGETING WRITING SKILLS YR 6 © PASCAL PRESS ISBN 9781925726299

Write an article discussing two points of view

Now you are ready to write a draft of your discussion to assist people when deciding whether to buy cage or free-range eggs.

Remember to:

- write a title as a question to identify the topic
- write an opening statement to introduce the topic and provide background information
- write a series of paragraphs to present arguments with evidence in favour of the topic
- write a series of paragraphs to present arguments with evidence against the topic
- write a conclusion and a recommendation
- use evaluative language to support both points of view
- write in present tense
- write in sentences with capital letters and full stops.

First draft

Write a draft of your discussion here.

Feedback

Ask your teacher, classmates or someone at home to suggest what you could do to improve your discussion.

Revised draft

Self-evaluation

I wrote
- ☐ a title as a question.
- ☐ an opening statement.
- ☐ a series of paragraphs in favour of the topic.
- ☐ a series of paragraphs against the topic.
- ☐ a conclusion and a recommendation.
- ☐ in present tense.

I used
- ☐ evaluative language to support both points of view.
- ☐ capital letters and full stops correctly in sentences.

TERM 2

REVIEW

COMPOUND SENTENCES

A **compound sentence** has two independent clauses joined by a conjunction such as for, and, nor, but, or, yet, so (FANBOYS). A comma is always written before the conjunction joining the two clauses.

1 **Write the correct FANBOYS conjunction to join these clauses.**

a One minute Oz was on the roadside, __________ the next minute he was in a spaceship.
b Oz had no idea where the robot was from, __________ did he know where it was going.
c The dust puffed up in a willy-willy, __________ there was no wind.
d Oz could stay and watch the spaceship, __________ he could run and get help.
e Oz stayed very quiet in the spaceship, __________ he would not be seen.
f The robot was from outer space, __________ it seemed to know what it was doing.
g Oz was surprised, __________ he didn't expect to see a spaceship near his home.

SENTENCES AND SENTENCE FRAGMENTS

If a group of words does not make sense on its own, it is not a sentence. It is a **sentence fragment**.

2 **Read these groups of words. Circle the verbs, if any, in each group. Remember, a verb may consist of one or more words.**

Write **S** if the group is a **sentence**. Write **F** if the group is a **fragment**. In each sentence you find, add the capital letter and full stop.

Example:

[S] Oz (was) confused when the spaceship (landed).
[ ] a 45,000 years ago
[ ] b many people in Papua New Guinea live in traditional communities
[ ] c New Zealand, Fiji, Indonesia
[ ] d fish farming in marine environments
[ ] e freshwater fish farming is cheap and efficient
[ ] f hens live in cages and are fed by machines

INFORMATIVE TEXT – Sociological report

A sociological report provides information about people, countries and cultures.

3 **Complete these notes about one of Australia's closest neighbours.**

Choose from these, but not the one you wrote about on page 24: New Zealand, Timor-Leste, Fiji, the Solomon Islands, New Caledonia, Indonesia, Singapore or Vanuatu.

Research the information in books, atlases or online.

Write in sentence fragments.

Country: ______________________________

Location: ______________________________

Climate: ______________________________

Population: ______________________________

Capital: ______________________________

Currency: ______________________________

Environment: ______________________________

 TARGETING WRITING SKILLS YR 6 © PASCAL PRESS ISBN 9781925726299

IMAGINATIVE TEXT – Science fiction

A narrative is often referred to as a 'story'. Narratives are usually fictitious or made up. They are written to entertain or amuse the reader.

Write another event that involves the characters from the science fiction story you wrote on page 29.

Plan

a How did your story end? ______________________________

____

b What will happen in this episode? ______________________________

____

c Will this episode continue the story, or will it be a flashback? ______________

Draft

____

____

____

____

____

____

____

PERSUASIVE TEXT – Discussion

The purpose of a discussion is to present different points of view about an issue. It allows the reader to think about different points of view before making an informed decision.

Every Friday night, Tami's family get a takeaway meal for dinner. Every week, they have a discussion about what meal they should get. It seems everyone has a different idea. Suggestions include: pizza, Indian, Thai, fish and chips, fried chicken and burgers.

5 Choose two takeaway options, perhaps your favourite and the favourite of another family member. Write the discussion that may take place when choosing the meal. Remember to introduce the topic with background information and write a recommendation to conclude the discussion.

Draft

____

____

____

____

____

____

____

GRAMMAR Complex sentences

A **clause** is a group of words with a subject and a verb. Sentences are constructed from clauses.

A **sentence** is a group of words that makes sense on its own. It always has a verb. It usually has a subject and often has an object.

A **simple sentence** has just one independent, or main, clause and one verb.

A **compound sentence** has two independent clauses joined by a conjunction.

A **complex sentence** is also constructed from two or more clauses. The clauses make connections between ideas.

In a complex sentence, there is one clause that tells the main idea. It is called the **main clause** or the **principal clause.** It makes sense on its own.

A **subordinate** or **dependent clause** gives more information about the main idea in the principal clause. Subordinate or dependent clauses may not make sense on their own.

Subordinate clauses are linked to the principal clause by a conjunction or a relative pronoun.

Conjunctions often used to join subordinate clauses:

after	when	although	so (that)	because	before
wherever	since	whenever	as	once	where
though	while	until	if	unless	whilst

Relative pronouns:

who	whom	whose	which	that

The conjunction or relative pronoun is at the beginning of the subordinate clause. A subordinate clause can occur at the beginning, the end or in the middle of a sentence. When it is in the middle of a sentence, it is called an **embedded clause.**

Example: *Papua New Guinea, which lies to the north of Australia, is Australia's nearest neighbour.*

Complex sentences may link ideas by providing a **reason** or **purpose.**

Example: *Oz was surprised because the robot seemed to know what it was doing.*

The subordinate clauses answer the question, "Why?"

Read these complex sentences. In each sentence, highlight the subordinating conjunction, circle the verbs in each clause, underline the main clause in green and underline the subordinate clause in red.

Example: *Oz was surprised* **because** *the robot seemed to know what it was doing.*

a Many people choose free-range eggs because the hens can go outside during the day.

b The farmers leave the shed doors open so (that) the hens can go outside.

c Since they are cheaper and the same nutritionally, many people choose cage eggs.

d Shoppers compare the prices of goods as they want the best value for money.

e Supermarkets position chocolate near the checkout so (that) customers will buy it.

TARGETING WRITING SKILLS YR 6 © PASCAL PRESS ISBN 9781925726299

GRAMMAR Complex sentences

Complex sentences may link ideas by expressing a condition or a concession.

Examples: *Supermarkets must not sell produce if it is past the use by date.*
It can be safe to eat food after the best by date unless it has spoiled.

Read these complex sentences. In each sentence, highlight the subordinating conjunction, circle the verbs in each clause, underline the main clause in green and underline the subordinate clause in red.

Example: *Supermarkets must not sell produce if it is past the use by date.*

a Unless it stops raining soon, the river will flood.
b Although they were prepared for the storm season, they didn't expect so much hail.
c The children always take an umbrella if it looks like rain.
d The family spends every day on the beach unless it is raining.

Complex sentences may link ideas by expressing a time relationship.

Examples: *Whenever I rub a balloon on my hair, my hair stands on end.*
Australia was made up of six separate colonies until they joined with one federal government.

Read these complex sentences. In each sentence, highlight the subordinating conjunction, circle the verbs in each clause, underline the main clause in green and underline the subordinate clause in red.

Example: *Whenever I rub a balloon on my hair, my hair stands on end.*

a The children played outside after the storm had blown over.
b The cook checked the use-by date before she cracked the eggs.
c Oz was hiding in the spaceship when the robot returned.
d Whenever I think of fish farming, I think of riding seahorses.

Add subordinate clauses to give more details about these simple sentences. Use one of the conjunctions from the box. Use as many different conjunctions as you can.

a Fish farming is good ____________________
b I like to watch science fiction movies ____________________
c I always brush my teeth ____________________
d I haven't been to the beach ____________________
e I will not buy the eggs ____________________
f Australia has had a national government ____________________
g The children stayed inside ____________________
h The robot came out of the spaceship ____________________
i Papua New Guinea was ruled by other countries ____________________
j The baker didn't make money from doughnuts ____________________

INFORMATIVE TEXTS Procedure

The purpose of a procedure is to give instructions, explain how to do something, tell how to get somewhere, or explain the rules to be followed.

Purpose: This procedure explains how to inflate a balloon without blowing.

Audience: The intended audience of this procedure is children who are learning about chemical changes.

Context: Texts like this would be found in science magazines, textbooks and online.

A procedure may include a photograph or illustrations to improve understanding.

A title identifies the purpose of the instructions.

How to Inflate a Balloon Without Blowing

An introductory statement may also be used to explain the goal or objective.

You may already be familiar with the way bicarb soda fizzes when vinegar is added. Now you can use that fizz to inflate a balloon.

Items required to complete the procedure are listed. Bullet points are often used.

Subheadings are used for each section.

Things you need

- bicarb soda
- vinegar
- a small plastic water bottle (make sure the neck is small enough for a balloon to fit on tightly)
- a funnel
- a balloon
- a teaspoon

A series of numbered steps tells what to do in order.

Each instruction is written as a command with the verb at the beginning. The subject 'you' is said to be understood.

Steps

1. Stretch the balloon a few times to make it softer and easier to inflate.
2. Pour vinegar into the bottle to half fill it.
3. Use a funnel to put 2 teaspoons of bicarb soda in the balloon.
4. Stretch the mouth of the balloon over the neck of the bottle so the bicarb soda falls into the vinegar.

As the gas, carbon dioxide, in the mixture rises, it will blow up the balloon.

A final statement concludes or explains the procedure.

Parts of Speech

Topic-related nouns and noun groups
- bicarb soda
- vinegar
- balloon
- funnel

Present tense action verbs
- stretch
- pour
- use

Prepositional phrases
- into the bottle
- in the balloon
- over the neck
- of the bottle
- into the vinegar
- in the mixture

TARGETING WRITING SKILLS YR 6 © PASCAL PRESS ISBN 9781925726299

Structure of a procedure

Title

The title of a procedure identifies the purpose of the instructions. It tells readers what the instructions refer to.

The title of this procedure is 'How to Inflate a Balloon Without Blowing'. Readers know they will be reading the instructions for inflating a balloon.

Circle the title of the procedure.

Introductory statements

Introductory statements may be used to explain the goal or objective.

Underline the statements that explain the goal or objective of the activity.

Subheadings

Subheadings are used to organise the information. There are two subheadings in this procedure.

a Highlight the subheadings.
b Write them here.

____

Language features of a procedure

Commands and action verbs

A command is a sentence that tells you what to do. It usually begins with a verb telling you the action you need to take.

In a command, the subject is left out. The subject is said to be understood. We know it is 'you'.

Example: *(You) Stretch the balloon a few times to make it softer and easier to inflate.*

a Reread the text. Draw a box around the action words that begin each command telling you what to do.
b Write the action words here.

____

Prepositional phrases

A **phrase** is a group of words that only makes sense in a sentence. It doesn't make sense on its own. It doesn't have a verb and it doesn't have a subject.

A **prepositional phrase** usually begins with a preposition and tells where a person or object is in space or time.

Example: *into* the bottle

In a procedure, prepositional phrases are necessary to tell where and when things should occur. If the *where* and *when* aren't followed, the procedure may not work as planned.

a Read the steps of the procedure. Highlight the prepositional phrases that tell you where or when to carry out the actions.
b Write the prepositions that begin each phrase here.

____

6 **Write prepositional phrases to complete these sentences.**

a Draw a picture ______________________________.
b Turn left ______________________________.
c Hold the balloon ______________________________.
d Put your plate ______________________________.

INFORMATIVE TEXTS Writing instructions for inflating a balloon

You can conduct a similar experiment using yeast, sugar and water to inflate a balloon without blowing, but you may need to be patient. It may take 20 minutes or more for the balloon to inflate.

Use what you know from the vinegar and bicarb soda procedure and this image to write the procedure for blowing up a balloon using yeast and sugar.

Plan

1. a Write a title for your procedure. ____________________

   b Write a statement to explain the goal or objective of your procedure.

   ____

2. **List the things that are required. Remember to use bullet points.**

   ____

   ____

   ____

   ____

   ____

3. **List the action words that you will use to tell others what to do.**

   ____

   ____

   ____

   ____

4. **Write the prepositional phrases that will help make your explanations clear.**

   ____

   ____

   ____

   ____

   ____

5. **List the steps that need to be followed to inflate a balloon without blowing.**

   1 ____________________

   2 ____________________

   3 ____________________

   4 ____________________

TARGETING WRITING SKILLS YR 6 © PASCAL PRESS ISBN 9781925726299

Draft

Now you are ready to write a procedure for using yeast, sugar and water to inflate a balloon without blowing.

Remember to:

- write a title for your procedure
- write an introductory statement to explain the goal or objective of your procedure
- use subheadings for each section
- list the things that are required, and remember to use bullet points
- write commands to explain what to do, and remember to number the instructions
- use present tense
- use prepositional phrases to tell where and when actions should occur
- write in sentences with capital letters and full stops.

First draft

Write a draft of your procedure here.

Feedback

Ask your teacher, classmates or someone at home to suggest what you could do to improve your procedure.

Revised draft

Self-evaluation

I wrote
- ☐ a title to identify the procedure.
- ☐ an introductory statement to explain the goal or objective of the procedure.
- ☐ commands to explain what to do.
- ☐ in present tense.
- ☐ in sentences with capital letters and full stops.

I used
- ☐ subheadings for each section.
- ☐ prepositional phrases to tell where and when actions should occur.
- ☐ bullet points to list items required.

I numbered
- ☐ the commands in order.

FOCUS ON IMAGINATIVE TEXTS Ballad

A ballad is a narrative or story written in rhyming verse. Like other narratives, ballads are written to entertain or amuse the reader. They have a beginning, a middle and an end with a complication and resolution.

Purpose: This ballad entertains with an amusing story about a dingo pup who explodes a rotten egg and thinks he's been shot by a bomb.

Audience: The intended audience of this ballad is anyone who enjoys funny stories told in ballad form.

Context: Ballads like this are found in collected works by the poet, anthologies, magazines, newspapers and online.

A ballad may be illustrated to aid interest and meaning.

The title introduces the topic or setting of the ballad.

The name of the poet is written below the title.

This ballad is written in four stanzas. Each stanza has four lines. The lines have an aabb rhyming pattern.

The first stanza introduces the setting and the characters.

The second and third stanzas identify the complication and other events.

The fourth stanza provides a resolution or end to the story.

High Explosive

by A. B. Banjo Paterson

'Twas the dingo pup to his dam that said,
"It's time I worked for my daily bread.
Out in the world I intend to go,
And you'd be surprised at the things I know.

"There's a wild duck's nest in a sheltered spot,
And I'll go right down and I'll eat the lot."
But when he got to his destined prey
He found that the ducks had flown away.

But an egg was left that would quench his thirst,
So he bit the egg and it straightway burst.
It burst with a bang, and he turned and fled,
For he thought that the egg had shot him dead.

"Oh, mother," he said, "let us clear right out
Or we'll lose our lives with the bombs about;
And it's lucky I am that I'm not blown up,
It's a very hard life," said the dingo pup.

Parts of Speech

Nouns and noun groups
- dingo pup
- dam
- daily bread
- wild duck's nest

Contractions
- 'twas
- it's
- you'd
- there's

Rhyme
- said/bread
- go/know
- spot/lot
- prey/away

Conjunctions
- and
- but
- so
- for

Direct speech
- said
- inverted commas

TARGETING WRITING SKILLS YR 6 © PASCAL PRESS ISBN 9781925726299

Structure of a ballad

Title

A ballad is an imaginative narrative or story written in rhyming verse. It has a title that provides a clue as to what the story is about. The title of this ballad *High Explosive* hints that something will explode in this story.

Circle the title of the ballad.

Poet

The name of the poet, if known, is written below the title.

Underline the poet's name.

Orientation

The first stanza introduces the setting and the characters.

Complete these details about the story.

a Who is the story about? ______________________________

b When does the story take place? ______________________________

c Where does the story take place? ______________________________

Complication

The complication is a problem that affects one or more of the characters.

Highlight the words in the text that answer these questions, then write the answers in your own words here.

a What did the pup set out to do?

____

b Why couldn't he achieve his goal?

____

c What did he decide to do instead?

____

d What happened then?

____

Resolution

The resolution occurs when the problem is solved or the story ends. The end of this story is amusing because of a misunderstanding.

Explain the misunderstanding that makes the story amusing.

____

Language features of a ballad

Rhythm and rhyme

This ballad rhymes in an aabb pattern, which means that the first two lines rhyme and the second two lines rhyme.

Use different colours to circle the pairs of rhyming words.

Apostrophes in contractions

Apostrophes are used to mark a missing letter or letters when two words are combined. Contractions can help to keep the rhythm in a ballad.
Examples: *'twas = it was, it's = it is, you'd = you would, there's = there is*

a Circle the contractions in the text.

b Write the contractions not already listed and the two words they represent here.

____

Note: Apostrophes are also used to show possession as in *duck's nest*.

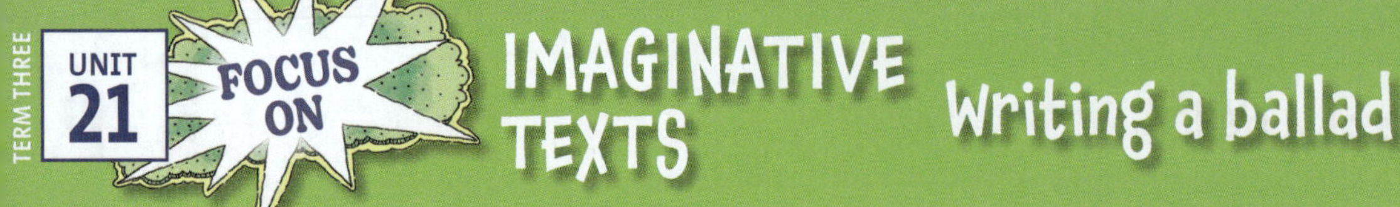

IMAGINATIVE TEXTS Writing a ballad

Write a ballad about another young Australian animal.

Plan

Plan your story before you write it in verse.

1. **Characters: List the characters who appear in your ballad.**

2. **Setting: Where does the story take place?**

3. **Goal:**
   a What is the character's goal?

   b How does the character attempt to achieve that goal?

4. **Complication: What happens to prevent the character from achieving the goal?**

5. **Resolution: How does the story end?**

6. **Now write an outline of your story in just a few sentences.**

7. **Circle words that you may be able to rhyme when you rewrite your story as a ballad.**

8. **Write the words and the words that rhyme with them on these lines.**

9. **Write a rhyming couplet (2 lines of verse that rhyme) to begin your ballad.**

10. **Write another rhyming couplet to include in your ballad.**

11. **Write a title for your ballad.**

TARGETING WRITING SKILLS YR 6 © PASCAL PRESS ISBN 9781925726299

Draft

Now you are ready to write a draft of the first stanza of your ballad.
Remember to:

- write the title of the ballad first
- write a stanza with four lines
- introduce the story setting including the characters, time and place
- use rhyming words at the ends of each pair of lines
- use contractions if necessary to help keep the rhythm
- begin each line with a capital letter
- end each sentence with a full stop.

First draft

Write a draft of the first stanza of your ballad here.

Feedback

Ask your teacher, classmates or someone at home to suggest what you could do to improve your ballad.

Revised draft

Self-evaluation

I wrote ☐ the title of the ballad first.
☐ a stanza with four lines.
I used ☐ rhyming words at the end of lines.
I kept ☐ the rhythm in my ballad.
I introduced ☐ the story setting.
I began ☐ each line with a capital letter.
I ended ☐ each sentence with a full stop.

PERSUASIVE TEXTS Advertising exposition

Advertising is a type of exposition. It promotes goods, services and activities. The aim is to persuade people to buy the goods, use the services or purchase access to the activities. Ads use positive words and images, are often visually appealing and use catchy slogans.

Purpose: This 1927 advertisement for *Oswald the Lucky Rabbit* convinces people to attend the cinema to watch the animated cartoon shorts created by Walt Disney for the Universal Pictures Corporation. Although the advertisement is almost one hundred years old, it has features of advertisements that are still in use today.

Audience: The intended audience of this poster is potential moviegoers.

Context: Texts like this would be found in newspapers and magazines, and online.

Advertisements are often illustrated with photos, cartoons or diagrams to catch the reader's attention.

Words are written in bold type or capital letters for emphasis.

Paragraphs use simple language to appeal to potential customers and explain why their product is the best.

A bold heading to catch attention. The heading is not always at the top of the advertisement.

A catchy slogan may be used to make it more memorable.

Parts of Speech

Topic-related nouns and noun groups
- rabbit
- shorts
- debut
- cartoon

Proper nouns
- Oswald
- Universal
- The Roxy
- Criterion

Sensational spelling
- krazy
- kartoon
- laffs
- kat

Emotive words and superlatives
- years of searching
- best
- biggest of them all
- loudest
- sensation
- super

 TARGETING WRITING SKILLS YR 6 © PASCAL PRESS ISBN 9781925726299

Structure of an advertising exposition

An advertising exposition, or advertisement, speaks directly to the audience and is written in strong emotive language that gets straight to the point. Although advertisements may vary in layout, they usually include features that are common to other persuasive texts.

Bold heading

A bold heading is used to catch the attention and tell the reader what is being advertised.

1 **Circle the heading of the advertisement.**

Arguments for the product

One or more paragraphs provide the audience with reasons for choosing the advertised product which, in this case, is cartoons that can be viewed at the cinema.

2
- **a** Underline the statements that tell readers why they should see the Oswald cartoons (shorts).
- **b** Write the reasons for seeing the cartoons here.

___

___

___

Slogan

A catchy slogan may be used to help people remember the product.

3
- **a** Highlight the slogan.
- **b** Write it here.

___

Language features of an advertising exposition

Emotive words and superlatives

In an advertisement, emotive words and superlatives, like *best* and *sensational*, are used to convince the potential customer to become an actual customer. They may exaggerate the product's benefits to snare a sale. This advertisement is trying to convince people to go to the movies to watch the Oswald cartoons.

Consider this statement: *Oswald Rabbit cartoons are funny*. It is not very compelling.

4 **The same message is repeated at least three times in the text. Write the statements here. Circle the superlatives and emotive words that try to convince you to go to the movies to watch Oswald.**

- **a** ___
- **b** ___
- **c** ___

Sensational spellings

Advertisements often use non-standard, or sensational, spellings to attract attention.

5
- **a** Highlight the sensational spellings in the text.
- **b** Write the sensational spellings and their correct, or standard, spelling here.

___

Synonyms

Synonyms are words with similar meanings. In advertisements, synonyms are often used to repeat a message without repeating the same words. Because this advertisement is almost 100 years old, some words may be unfamiliar to a modern audience.

6
- **a** Circle words with meanings of which you are unsure.
- **b** Research their meanings.
- **c** Choose two of the words. Write the words and synonyms for them here.

___

FOCUS ON

PERSUASIVE TEXTS Writing an advertising exposition

Imagine a character you would like to see in an animated movie.
Write an advertisement for that character and animated movie.

Before you start

Look at posters advertising animated movies that are currently available. Choose the poster that you find the most compelling. Write the features that you observe.

1 **What features of the headline make it eye-catching; for example: colour, font, size.**

2 **List emotive words and superlatives that are used in the advertisement.**

3 **If the movie has a catchy slogan, write it here.**

4 **List other features of the advertisement that make it compelling.**

Plan

Now you are ready to plan an advertisement for your own imaginary character.

5 **Draw the character in a scene from your animated movie here.**

6 **What is the name of the character?**

7 **What is the title of the movie?**

8 **What genre is the movie? For example, is it scary, funny, science fiction or fantasy?**

9 **Write emotive words and superlatives to convince moviegoers to see your movie.**

10 **List some sensational spellings you could use.**

11 **Write a slogan for your movie or movie character.**

12 **What strategies will you use to make the heading of your poster eye-catching?**

 TARGETING WRITING SKILLS YR 6 © PASCAL PRESS ISBN 9781925726299

Draft

Now you are ready to write a draft of your advertising exposition.
Remember to:

- write a bold, catchy heading
- write short paragraphs to tell about the movie or character
- use emotive words and superlatives to convince people to watch your movie
- include sensational spellings of some words
- write a catchy slogan to make your character memorable
- use capital letters for proper nouns.

First draft

Write a draft of your advertisement here.

Feedback

Ask your teacher, classmates or someone at home to suggest what you could do to improve your advertisement.

Revised draft

Self-evaluation

I wrote ☐ a bold, catchy heading.
☐ short paragraphs to tell about the movie or character.
☐ a catchy slogan.
I included ☐ sensational spellings.
I used ☐ emotive words and superlatives.
☐ capital letters for proper nouns.

UNIT 24 FOCUS ON

RECREATING TEXTS Ballad

A ballad is a narrative or story written in rhyming verse. Ballads have a beginning, a middle and an end with a complication and resolution.

Purpose: This excerpt from *Benjamin Bandicoot* by Banjo Paterson is a poem, not a ballad. It doesn't tell a story. Its purpose is to help us understand and appreciate bandicoots.

Audience: The intended audience of this poem is anyone who enjoys poetry about nature.

Context: Poems like this are found in collected works by the poet, anthologies, magazines, newspapers and online.

Read these two verses from the poem *Benjamin Bandicoot* in which Banjo Paterson describes a bandicoot.

Write a narrative, that could form the basis of a ballad, to tell what you would see and how you would respond if you came across a bandicoot in its native habitat.

Benjamin Bandicoot

by A. B. Banjo Paterson

If you walk in the bush at night,
In the wonderful silence deep,
By the flickering lantern light
When the birds are all asleep
You may catch a sight of old Skinny-go-root,
Otherwise Benjamin Bandicoot.

With a snout that can delve and dig,
With claws that are strong as steel,
He roots like a pigmy pig
To get his evening meal,
For creeping creatures and worms and roots
Are highly relished by bandicoots.

Plan

Plan your story before you write it in verse.

1. **Characters: You and the bandicoot. Are there any others?**

___

2. **Setting: Describe the location, including sights and sounds.**

___

3. **Goal: Why are you there?**

___

4. **What draws your attention to the bandicoot?**

___

5. **How do you react?**

___

6. **Now write an outline of the story in just a few sentences.**

___

___

7. **Write a rhyming couplet (2 lines of verse that rhyme) to begin your ballad.**

___

___

TARGETING WRITING SKILLS YR 6 © PASCAL PRESS ISBN 9781925726299

Draft

Now you are ready to write a draft of the first stanza of your ballad.

Remember to:

- write the title of the ballad first
- write a stanza with four lines
- introduce the story setting, including the characters, time and place
- use rhyming words at the ends of each pair of lines
- use contractions if necessary to help keep the rhythm
- begin each line with a capital letter
- end each sentence with a full stop.

First draft

Write a draft of the first stanza of your ballad here.

Feedback

Ask your teacher, classmates or someone at home to suggest what you could do to improve your ballad.

Revised draft

Self-evaluation

I wrote ☐ the title of the ballad first.
☐ a stanza with four lines.
I introduced ☐ the story setting.
I used ☐ rhyming words at the end of lines.
I kept ☐ the rhythm in my ballad.
I began ☐ each line with a capital letter.
I ended ☐ each sentence with a full stop.

TERM 3 REVIEW

COMPLEX SENTENCES

A complex sentence has two or more clauses, including a main clause and one or more subordinate clauses. Subordinate clauses are linked to the principal clause by a conjunction or a relative pronoun.

1 Read these complex sentences. In each sentence, highlight the subordinating conjunction, circle the verbs in each clause, underline the main clause in green and underline the subordinate clause in red.

Example: We waited for twenty minutes *until* the balloon was inflated.

- **a** We stretch the balloon over the bottle so (that) the bicarb soda falls into the water.
- **b** The dingo pup left home because he wanted to find his own food.
- **c** If you like funny cartoons, you will love Oswald the Lucky Rabbit.
- **d** You might see a bandicoot when you are walking in the bush at night.
- **e** Although it was expensive, people queued for hours to buy the latest watch.

2 Add subordinate clauses to give more details about these simple sentences. Use one of these conjunctions: unless, as, since, before, after, wherever.

- **a** The children closed the windows ______________________.
- **b** The spectators cheered ______________________.
- **c** It will not be possible to go to the beach ______________________
- **d** His little sister followed him ______________________.
- **e** I left home ______________________.
- **f** You may not have another apple ______________________.

INFORMATIVE TEXT – Procedure

A procedure gives instructions or explains how to do something. Procedures usually have an introductory statement to explain the goal or objective, a list of materials required and a series of numbered steps to follow. This procedure explains how to make a mini fountain.

Make a Mini Fountain

Make a mini fountain in your drinking cup. This activity can be messy so do it outside.

Things you need

- a reusable drinking cup with a tight lid and its own straw
- a teaspoon
- bicarb soda
- vinegar
- a small amount of plasticene or modelling clay

Did you notice that the numbered steps were missing from the procedure?

3
- **a** Use your knowledge of bicarb soda and vinegar from the procedure on page 40.
- **b** Write the steps of the procedure here. Remember to number them.

____

____

____

____

____

TARGETING WRITING SKILLS YR 6 © PASCAL PRESS ISBN 9781925726299

IMAGINATIVE TEXT – Ballad

A ballad is a narrative or story written in rhyming verse. Ballads have a beginning, a middle and an end with a complication and resolution. While you may know *Waltzing Matilda* as a song, it was first written as a ballad to tell a story. Some words were changed to fit it to the music.

Waltzing Matilda

by A. B. Banjo Paterson

Oh! There once was a swagman camped in a Billabong,
Under the shade of a Coolabah tree;
And he sang as he looked at his old billy boiling,
"Who'll come a-waltzing Matilda with me?"

Down came a jumbuck to drink at the water-hole,
Up jumped the swagman and grabbed him with glee;
And he sang as he stowed him away in his tucker-bag,
"You'll come a-waltzing Matilda with me."

4 **Rewrite the story told in these first two stanzas of the ballad in your own words. Your story should include the setting (characters, location, time), goal and an event.**

____

____

____

____

____

____

____

PERSUASIVE TEXT – Advertising exposition

An advertising exposition, or advertisement, speaks directly to the audience and is written in strong emotive language that gets straight to the point. Although advertisements may vary in layout, they usually include features that are common to other persuasive texts.

5 **Think about a favourite animated character from a movie or video game. Plan a poster advertising the character and the movie or game the character appears in.**
Remember to use features common to advertisements, including an eye-catching heading, emotive words, images and a catchy slogan.

GRAMMAR Complex sentences

A complex sentence is constructed from two or more clauses. The clauses make connections between ideas. One clause tells the main idea. It is called the **main clause** or the **principal clause**. It makes sense on its own.

A **subordinate** or **dependent clause** gives more information about the main idea. It may not make sense on its own. Subordinate clauses are linked to the principal clause by a conjunction or a relative pronoun.

Conjunctions often used to join subordinate clauses:

after	as	although	unless	before	though
because	whilst	if	once	when	where
so (that)	since	whenever	while	wherever	until

Relative pronouns:

who	whom	whose	which	that

The conjunction or relative pronoun is at the beginning of the subordinate clause. A subordinate clause can occur at the beginning, the end or in the middle of a sentence. When it is in the middle of another clause, it is called an **embedded clause**.

Example: *The robot, who appeared out of the spaceship, hovered away over the trees.*

The relative pronouns **who** and **whom** are used when talking about people.

The relative pronouns **which** and **that** are used when talking about animals and things.

Example: *The people, who voted against the referendum, wanted to remain a monarchy.*

Example: *The dingo pup, that left home to seek his fortune, was scared by an explosive egg.*

The possessive **whose** is used for people, animals and things.

Example: *The bandicoot, whose babies were still in the pouch, was looking for food.*

Example: *The girl, whose hair was standing on end, had rubbed it with a balloon.*

Subordinate clauses that begin with a relative pronoun are adjectival clauses. They do the work of adjectives and give more information about nouns. They always follow the noun they describe.

In these complex sentences, circle the relative pronoun, underline the adjectival clause and highlight the noun that the clause describes.

Example: *The baker, who made delicious doughnuts, was pleased with the sales.*

a Sir Henry Parkes, who was an Australian politician, delivered the Tenterfield Oration.

b Oz was surprised by the spaceship that landed nearby.

c The fisherman gave some fish to the children whom he met on the jetty.

Add adjectival clauses to these main clauses to make complex sentences. Use a relative pronoun to begin the clause. Remember, the clauses always follow the noun they describe.

a The hen laid an egg every day.

____

b The movie was the best this year.

____

c The student made a fountain using bicarb soda and vinegar.

____

TARGETING WRITING SKILLS YR 6 © PASCAL PRESS ISBN 9781925726299

Many subordinate clauses do the work of adverbs. They give more information about the verbs and are called adverbial clauses.
They are joined to the principal clause using a conjunction and tell us how, when, where, why or for how long things happen.

Example: *The customer chose free-range eggs because the hens weren't caged.*

In these complex sentences, circle the conjunction, underline the adverbial clause and highlight the verb about which the clause gives more information.

Example: *The robot left the spaceship while Oz was watching it.*

- a Although free-range eggs are often more expensive, many people buy them.
- b I go fishing with my father whenever he takes the boat out.
- c The girl rubbed her hair with a balloon so that it would stick out all over.
- d After the storm had past, they saw a brilliant double rainbow.

Complex sentences have one main clause and one or more subordinate clauses. The subordinate clauses may be adjectival clauses and give more information about a noun, or they may be adverbial clauses and give more information about a verb.

Some complex sentences have one or more adjectival clauses and one or more adverbial clauses. Example: *Sir Henry Parkes, who was a colonial Australian politician, delivered the Tenterfield Oration because he was in favour of federation.*
The principal clause is: *Sir Henry Parkes delivered the Tenterfield Oration.*
The adjectival clause tells more about Parkes: *who was a colonial Australian politician.*
The adverbial clause tells why he delivered the speech: *because he was in favour of federation.*

In these complex sentences, highlight the principal clause, underline each subordinate clause in a different colour, and circle the conjunction or relative pronoun that links the clauses.

Example: *Sir Henry Parkes, who was a colonial Australian politician, delivered the Tenterfield Oration because he was in favour of federation.*

- a The wild duck's nest, which was hidden in a sheltered spot, was empty because the ducks had flown away.
- b Static electricity, which is a build-up of charge on the surface of an object, is not like current electricity which flows through a circuit.
- c You may have experienced static electricity if you were zapped by a door handle after you crossed a carpeted floor.
- d A constellation, that had an arrow pointing to a star, was stamped on the crate.

When composing text, writers often use a combination of simple, compound and complex sentences. They may vary sentence beginnings to make the text flow and to add interest.

Read the following text. Circle the verbs. Put brackets [ ] around the simple sentences. Underline the compound sentences and highlight any complex sentences.

Adaptation to climate change

Adaptation is possible. Some types of coral on the Great Barrier Reef have adapted to warmer water temperatures. Coral need algae to survive, but warm water and intense sunlight kill the algae. Well-adapted corals produce a sunscreen-like substance that shields algae from the heat. Corals without this adaptation are likely to die off as seas get warmer.

Source: *Adaptation* by Janette Ellis, Go Facts, Blake Education.

INFORMATIVE TEXTS Historical recount

The purpose of a historical recount is to tell what happened in chronological order — the time order in which events occurred.

Purpose: This historical recount documents a series of events which led to the Federation of Australia in 1901.

Audience: The intended audience of this historical recount is children who are learning about, and others who are interested in, the history of Australia.

Context: Texts like this would be found in history books, magazines and online.

Historical recounts often include photographs or illustrations.

The title identifies the topic.

The orientation gives details about what, when and where.

A series of paragraphs recounts events in chronological order.

A concluding paragraph finalises the recount and links back to the orientation.

Australia Becomes a Federation

Before Federation, Australia did not have one unified government. Each colony had its own government.

Although the idea of a government for all Australia was suggested by Sir Henry Parkes in 1867, progress was slow until 1889. In that year, two events helped move Australia towards Federation. The first was a report by Major-General J. Bevan Edwards who suggested that Australia needed a national army to protect itself. Sir Henry Parkes reiterated the need in his famous speech at Tenterfield later that year.

From 1890, delegates from the colonies met to draft a constitution. When the draft was complete, referendums were held in 1898 and 1899 to gain approval from the people. After that, it was necessary for the British Government and Monarch to also agree.

On 17 September 1900, Queen Victoria proclaimed that the Commonwealth of Australia would become a Federation on 1 January 1901.

Parts of Speech

Topic-related nouns and noun groups
- Federation
- one unified government
- colony
- a government for all Australia
- progress
- two events

Proper nouns
- Australia
- Sir Henry Parkes
- Major-General J. Bevan Edwards
- Tenterfield

Proper adjectives
- British

Past tense
- did not have
- had
- was suggested
- helped
- reiterated

Adverbial phrases
- before Federation
- in 1867
- until 1889
- later that year
- from 1890

TARGETING WRITING SKILLS YR 6 © PASCAL PRESS ISBN 9781925726299

Structure of a historical recount

Title

The title of a historical recount identifies the topic.

1 **Circle the title of the historical recount.**

Orientation

The orientation gives details about what, when and where.

2 **Highlight the orientation.**

Series of paragraphs

A series of paragraphs recounts details in order. Each paragraph recounts events that led to the Federation of Australia in 1901.

3 **Underline the statements that tell about events leading to Federation. Write notes about the years and the events.**

a ______________________________

b ______________________________

c ______________________________

d ______________________________

e ______________________________

Concluding paragraph

A concluding paragraph finalises the recount and links back to the orientation.

4 **Highlight the statement that links back to the orientation.**

Language features of a historical recount

Nouns and noun groups

A **noun group** is a group of words built around a noun. It usually begins with a **determiner** and may contain other words that give more information about **the key noun**. A **determiner** is a word that introduces the noun group.

Examples: ***one** unified government*, ***the** first*, ***his** famous speech*

5 **Write four noun groups, found in the text but not already listed, on these lines. Highlight the determiner in each group.**

____

Proper nouns

Proper nouns are the special names of people, places, objects and events. Example: *Australia*

If a proper noun consists of more than one word, the important words are capitalised.

Example: *Commonwealth of Australia*

6 **Circle all the proper nouns in the text.**

Adverbial phrases

Adverbial phrases provide more information about how, when, where, why or for how long things happen. In a historical recount, they are used to sequence and link events over time.

Example: *before Federation*

7 **a** Use a different colour to highlight the adverbial phrases that tell when things happened in the text.

b List the prepositions that introduce the adverbial phrases that tell when things happened.

____

TERM FOUR

UNIT 27

FOCUS ON

INFORMATIVE TEXTS Writing a historical recount

The constitution is a set of rules that tells how Australia should be governed. The constitution can only be changed through a referendum. A referendum is a yes/no question on which the people of Australia vote.

Use these notes to write a historical recount of referendums in Australia. You may refer to other materials such as books and online sources if you wish.

Since Federation: 19 referendums, 44 questions, 8 changes to the constitution

Successful referendums:

1906 – allowed elections for both houses of parliament to be held together

1910 – gave Federal Government power to take over state debt

1928 – ended per capita payments to states and established a loan council to oversee state borrowing

1946 – gave Australian Government power over social welfare payments

1967 – gave Australian Government powers to make special laws for Aboriginal and Torres Strait Islander peoples, and that they be counted in the census

1977 – required that:

- a casual senate seat be filled by a person from the same party for the term's duration
- people living in territories as well as states vote in referendums
- a retiring age be set for judges of federal courts

Plan

1. **Write a title to introduce the topic of your historical recount.**

___

2. **Write an orientation that gives details about what, when and where.**

___

___

3. **Write some adverbial phrases you will use to provide information about when the referendums and changes took place.**

___

___

4. **Write some noun groups you will use in your recount. Highlight the determiner in each group.**

___

___

___

5. **Write a statement to conclude the recount and link back to the orientation.**

___

___

TARGETING WRITING SKILLS YR 6 © PASCAL PRESS ISBN 9781925726299

Draft

Now you are ready to write a historical recount about referendums in Australia.
Remember to:

- write the title to introduce the topic first
- write an orientation to give details about what, when and where
- write a series of paragraphs that recounts events in chronological order
- write a concluding paragraph to finalise the recount and link back to the orientation
- use adverbial phrases to tell when things happened
- use past tense
- use capital letters for proper nouns and proper adjectives
- write in sentences with capital letters and full stops.

First draft

Write a draft of your historical recount here.

Feedback

Ask your teacher, classmates or someone at home to suggest what you could do to improve your historical recount.

Revised draft

Self-evaluation

I wrote
- ☐ the title on the first line.
- ☐ an orientation to give details about what, when and where.
- ☐ a series of paragraphs to recount events in chronological order.
- ☐ a concluding paragraph to finalise the recount and link to the orientation.
- ☐ in past tense.

I used
- ☐ adverbial phrases to tell when things happened.
- ☐ capital letters for proper nouns and proper adjectives.
- ☐ capital letters and full stops correctly in sentences.

IMAGINATIVE TEXTS Limericks

A limerick is a short, funny, rhyming poem with a singsong rhythm that makes it easy to remember and recite. All limericks are five lines long and follow the same structure. The purpose of a limerick is to entertain and amuse.

Purpose: These limericks entertain and amuse people of all ages.

Audience: The intended audience of these limericks is people of any age who enjoy funny poems.

Context: Poems like these are often included in anthologies and magazines for children.

The title of a limerick, if one is provided, is usually the first line of the limerick.

The first line is the orientation. It tells who the limerick is about and something about them.

Lines 2, 3 and 4 tell the story events and complication.

The last line concludes the limerick and is usually funny.

Lines 1, 2 and 5 have three beats each and rhyme with one another.

Lines 3 and 4 have two beats each and rhyme with each other.

Three Limericks by Edward Lear

There was an Old Man with a Beard

There was an Old Man with a beard,
Who said, "It is just as I feared! –
Two Owls and a Hen,
Four Larks and a Wren,
Have all built their nests in my beard."

There was an Old Man in a Tree

There was an Old Man in a tree,
Who was horribly bored by a Bee;
When they said, "Does it buzz?"
He replied, "Yes, it does!
It's a regular brute of a Bee!"

There was an Old Man in a Barge

There was an Old Man in a barge,
Whose nose was exceedingly large;
But in fishing by night,
It supported a light,
Which helped that Old Man in a barge.

Language features of limericks

Rhyming words
- beard/feared
- hen/wren
- tree/bee
- buzz/does

Expanded noun groups
- an Old Man with a beard
- an Old Man in a tree
- an Old Man in a barge

Adjectives and adjectival phrases
- old
- with a beard
- two
- regular

Past tense
- was
- said
- have built

Direct speech
- said
- inverted commas

TARGETING WRITING SKILLS YR 6 © PASCAL PRESS ISBN 9781925726299

Structure of a limerick

Title

A limerick doesn't always have a title. If a limerick does have a title, it is usually the first line. Titles may be used in an anthology in the contents or index to make the limerick easier to find.

Circle the titles of the three limericks.

Orientation

The first line usually begins with a person and something about the person such as the name, a physical feature, or where the person is from. Note that it is the same as the title.

Highlight the first line of each limerick.

Story events and complication

Lines 2, 3 and 4 (and sometimes 5) tell the story events and complication.

In your own words, explain the complication in each limerick.

Limerick 1: ____________________

Limerick 2: ____________________

Limerick 3: ____________________

Conclusion

The fifth line concludes the limerick. It is usually humorous.

In your own words, explain the humour in the limerick.

Limerick 1: ____________________

Limerick 2: ____________________

Limerick 3: ____________________

Language features of a limerick

Rhyme

Limericks have a set rhyming structure. Lines 1, 2 and 5 rhyme with each other. Lines 3 and 4 rhyme with each other. Sometimes, as occurs in these three limericks, the fifth line repeats a word from line 1 or 2.

Use different colours to circle the words that rhyme in each limerick.

Expanded noun groups

In a limerick, noun groups are expanded with adjectives, adjectival phrases and adjectival clauses to give more information about the **key noun**. The first line is the principal clause. It introduces the main idea and the key noun, *man*. The second line is a subordinate clause, in this case an adjectival clause, that begins with the relative pronoun *who* to give more information about the *man*.

Adjective example: *old*

Adjectival phrase example: *with a beard*

Adjectival clause example: *Who was horribly bored by a Bee.*

Underline the adjectives, adjectival phrases and adjectival clauses in each limerick. (Avoid underlining adverbial phrases which tell where, when, how or why.)

Writing a limerick

Write your own limerick. While the three limericks here are about an Old Man, limericks can be about anyone, but usually someone with an unusual characteristic, name or from an unusual place.

Plan

1 **Who will your limerick be about?**

___

2 **What will make your character unique? Brainstorm ideas for:**

a names – ___

b features – ___

c locations – ___

Circle your favourite idea.

3 **What will happen to your character (events and complication)? Brainstorm ideas. Circle your favourite idea.**

___

___

4 **How will your limerick conclude? Brainstorm ideas. Circle your favourite idea.**

___

___

5 **Draw a picture to illustrate your limerick.**

The first line of a limerick, the orientation, is easiest to write. It introduces the character and what makes them unique. It always begins with the words *There was a/an*.

6 **Write the first line of your limerick here.**

___

7 a Write the last word of your first line and words that rhyme with it.

___

b Circle the words that may be the best fit for your limerick.

8 **Write phrases ending with those rhyming words. Circle your favourite phrase.**

___

___

9 a Write an event or complication that will occur in your limerick.

___

b Circle the key words.

c Write words that rhyme with the key words.

___

TARGETING WRITING SKILLS YR 6 © PASCAL PRESS ISBN 9781925726299

Draft

Now you are ready to write a draft of your limerick.
Remember to:

- write the first line beginning with *There was a/an*
- begin the second line with *Who* and write an adjectival clause
- include a complication or event
- include a humorous conclusion
- ensure lines 1, 2 and 5 rhyme
- ensure lines 3 and 4 rhyme.

First draft

Write a draft of your limerick here.

Feedback

Ask your teacher, classmates or someone at home to suggest what you could do to improve your limerick.

Revised draft

Self-evaluation

I began ☐ the limerick with There was a/an.
☐ the second line with Who.

I included ☐ a complication or event.
☐ a humorous conclusion.

I ensured ☐ lines 1, 2 and 5 rhymed.
☐ lines 3 and 4 rhymed.

PERSUASIVE TEXTS Movie review

A movie review is written to summarise and analyse a movie. It provides the audience with background information, a summary of the plot and descriptions of the characters.

Purpose: This text reviews the movie *Rabbit-Proof Fence.*

Audience: The intended audience of this movie review is others who enjoy watching movies and may be looking for a historical movie, set in Australia.

Context: Texts like this would be found in newspapers and magazines, and online.

A movie review may be accompanied by a photograph of the movie poster.

A heading identifies the title of the movie. Each word of the title is capitalised.

Rabbit-Proof Fence

The name of the director and the release date are also noted.

Director: Phillip Noyce
Released: February 2002
Based on a true story.

The opening paragraph introduces the setting and the main idea of the movie.

The movie, which is set in Western Australia in 1931, is about three Aboriginal girls. The girls are stolen from their mothers and taken to live in a settlement over two thousand kilometres away.

Additional paragraphs provide more information about story events, characters and themes of the movie.

The girls are treated harshly at the settlement, forced to forget their culture and not permitted to speak their own language. They escape and make an arduous journey home, following the rabbit-proof fence.

About family, love and belonging, the movie is highly emotive. We cannot help but feel pain at the injustice the girls experience. We also fear for their safety on their epic journey. However, we must also admire their determination, resourcefulness and resilience.

In a final statement, the writer gives an overall opinion of the movie and a recommendation.

I recommend this movie for adults and children over 11 years who enjoy adventure stories, and especially those who wish to gain a better understanding of Australia's history.

WARNING: This movie may contain names, images or voices of deceased Aboriginal and Torres Strait Islander peoples.

Parts of Speech

Topic-related nouns and noun groups
- Western Australia
- three Indigenous Australian girls
- a settlement over two thousand kilometres away

Proper nouns
- Rabbit-Proof Fence
- Phillip Noyce
- February
- Western Australia

Proper adjectives
- Indigenous Australian

Present tense
- is
- are stolen
- are treated
- escape

Emotive and evaluative language
- cannot help but feel pain
- injustice
- fear
- admire
- recommend

Connectives
- however

TARGETING WRITING SKILLS YR 6 © PASCAL PRESS ISBN 9781925726299

Structure of a movie review

Heading
The heading identifies the title of the movie being reviewed. Each word is capitalised.

1 **Circle the title.**

Below the title, the name of the director and the year of the movie's release are noted. This review also tells you that the movie is based on a true story. This information can usually be found with an internet search.

2 **Underline the name of the director and the year the movie was released.**

Setting
The opening paragraph tells where and when the movie takes place and who it is about.

3 **Underline the words that tell you about the setting. Write them here.**

Where: ______________________________

When: ______________________________

Who: ______________________________

Main events
A series of paragraphs tells the main events. There are four main events in this story.

4 a Circle the words that tell the four main events.
b Write them here.

____

Recommendation
In the final paragraph, the writer provides a judgement and recommendation.

5 **Highlight the recommendation.**

Language features of a movie review

Emotive and evaluative language
The writer tells us that the movie is highly emotive. The writer then tells us what emotions we may expect to feel.

6 **Use a different colour to highlight the emotions.**

7 **In an evaluation of the movie, the writer makes a recommendation. Who does the writer recommend the movie for?**

____

8 **The review also contains a warning. Who is the warning intended for?**

____

Nouns and noun groups
A **noun group** is a group of words built around a key noun to give more information about it. Examples: ***the** movie, **three** Aboriginal girls, **an** arduous journey home*

9 **Write four noun groups, not already listed, on these lines. Highlight the determiner in each group.**

____

Proper nouns
Proper nouns are the special names of people, places, objects and events, including movies and books. The important words in proper nouns are capitalised. Example: *Western Australia.*

10 **Put brackets [ ] around all the proper nouns in the text.**

PERSUASIVE TEXTS

Writing a movie review

Write a review of a movie you have seen recently. If possible, choose another movie that is set in Australia and based on a true story.

Examples:

Oddball, directed by Stuart McDonald, released 2015

The Dish, directed by Rob Sitch, released in 2000

Red Dog, directed by Kriv Stenders, released in 2011

Penguin Bloom, directed by Glendyn Ivin, released in 2020

Let your readers know who the movie is about, where and when it is set and what happens in it.

Draw a picture or paste a photo of the poster for the movie you are reviewing here.

Plan

Make notes to plan your review.

1. **Movie title:** ______
   Director: ______
   Year of release: ______
   Characters: ______
   Setting (place and time): ______
2. **Is the movie based on a true event?** ______
3. **What are the main story events? Write notes in sentence fragments.**
   ______
   ______
   ______
4. **What are the themes of the movie?**
   ______
   ______
5. **What emotions might movie viewers expect to feel while watching the movie?**
   ______
6. **Write a statement to give your overall opinion of the movie and who you would recommend it for.**
   ______

TARGETING WRITING SKILLS YR 6 © PASCAL PRESS ISBN 9781925726299

Draft

Now you are ready to write a draft of your movie review.

Remember to:

- write the title as a heading
- write information about the director, the year of the movie's release and whether the movie is based on a true story
- write an opening paragraph to introduce the setting
- write additional paragraphs to give more details about story events and themes
- write a final judgement of the movie, including a recommendation
- use capital letters for the movie title and other proper nouns
- use capital letters and full stops correctly in sentences.

First draft

Write a draft of your movie review here.

Feedback

Ask your teacher, classmates or someone at home to suggest what you could do to improve your movie review.

Revised draft

Self-evaluation

I wrote ☐ the title as a heading.
☐ an opening paragraph to introduce the setting.
☐ a judgement and recommendation.
I identified ☐ the director and year of release.
I gave ☐ more details about story events and themes.
I capitalised ☐ proper nouns.
I used ☐ capital letters and full stops correctly in sentences.

TERM FOUR

UNIT 32 FOCUS ON

RECREATING TEXTS Movie review

A movie review is written to summarise and analyse a movie. It provides the audience with background information, a summary of the plot and descriptions of the characters.

Purpose: The purpose of this text is to review the movie, *Storm Boy*.

Audience: The intended audience of this movie review is others who enjoy watching movies that are about animals and set in Australia.

Context: Texts like this would be found in newspapers and magazines, and online.

Storm Boy is a movie based on a book of the same name by Colin Thiele. It is about Mike, a ten-year-old boy, who grows up on an isolated beach in South Australia. He rescues three orphaned pelicans. An Aboriginal man, named Fingerbone, helps him look after the pelicans. When the pelicans are released, two fly away and are not seen again. The third, Mr Percival, returns, and he and Mike form a strong and lasting friendship.

The movie, directed by Shawn Seet and starring Finn Little, Geoffrey Rush and Trevor Jamieson, was released in 2019.

Read the following comments made by movie goers who watched the movie, *Storm Boy*, and use them to write a review of the movie. If you have watched the movie, you may add your own comments and recommendation.

"Great movie for children over 8 years" "Not scary" "Made me cry"

"Very sentimental" "Bleak" "Heartwarming" "Predictable"

"I like the environmental theme. We need to look after our wildlife."

"Mike was lucky he didn't have to go to school. But he would have been lonely without friends his age."

"I felt sad for Mike that his Mum died." "The scenery is beautiful."

"Pelicans are very unusual birds, but I like them." "A waste of time"

"People who love animal movies will love Storm Boy."

"An old-fashioned family movie" "Pointless and disappointing"

"I don't like animals being hunted." "Believable — I felt I was there."

Plan

Make notes to plan your review.

1 **Movie title:** ______

Director: ______

Year of release: ______

Characters: ______

Setting (place and time): ______

2 **What are the themes of the movie?**

______

3 **Highlight words in the comments that will help you describe the emotions that viewers will feel.**

4 **Write a recommendation about who should watch the movie and why.**

______

Write a movie review

Now you are ready to write a review of the movie, *Storm Boy*.
Remember to:

- write the title as a heading
- write information about the director and the year of the movie's release
- write an opening paragraph to introduce the setting
- write additional paragraphs to give more details about story events and themes
- write a final judgement of the movie, including a recommendation
- use capital letters for the movie title and other proper nouns
- use capital letters and full stops correctly in sentences.

First draft

Write a draft of your movie review here.

Feedback

Ask your teacher, classmates or someone at home to suggest what you could do to improve your movie review.

Revised draft

Self-evaluation

I wrote ☐ the title as a heading.
☐ an opening paragraph to introduce the setting.
☐ a judgement and recommendation.
I identified ☐ the director and year of release.
I gave ☐ more details about story events and themes.
I capitalised ☐ proper nouns.
I used ☐ capital letters and full stops correctly in sentences.

TERM 4

REVIEW

COMPLEX SENTENCES

A **complex sentence** is constructed from two or more clauses. One is a **main clause** or **principal clause**. It makes sense on its own. The others are **subordinate** or **dependent clauses** that give more information about the main idea and are linked to the principal clause by a conjunction or a relative pronoun. The conjunction or relative pronoun is at the beginning of the subordinate clause. Subordinate clauses can occur at the beginning, the end or in the middle of a sentence.

In these complex sentences, highlight the principal clause, underline each subordinate clause in a different colour, and circle the conjunction or relative pronoun that links the clauses.

Example: Sir Henry Parkes, who was an early Australian politician, delivered a speech at Tenterfield because he wanted Australia to become a Federation.

- **a** Queen Victoria, who was the ruling monarch, proclaimed Australia a Federation because the people had voted in favour of it.
- **b** Since Australia became a Federation in 1901, there have been 19 referendums which have led to eight changes to the constitution.
- **c** In the first referendum, which was held in 1906, the people agreed that both houses of parliament could be elected at the same time.
- **d** A limerick is a short, funny, rhyming poem that is written to entertain and amuse.
- **e** The old man, who had a big, bushy beard, went to the barber because animals started to nest in it.
- **f** The movie, which is about three Aboriginal girls who were stolen from their mothers, is called *Rabbit-Proof Fence*.
- **g** The girls, who escaped from the settlement, followed the rabbit-proof fence until they were reunited with their mothers.
- **h** The movie, *Storm Boy*, is not recommended for really young children because they may be sad when the hunters shoot the pelicans.

INFORMATIVE TEXT – Historical recount

A historical recount tells about historical events in chronological order.

Use these notes to write a history of voting in Australia.

Voting in Australia

- before 1850s governors were appointed, military officers
- 1850s voting began in colonies, but not everyone could vote
- 1856 secret ballot, known as 'Australian ballot' introduced in some colonies
- 1901 Federation of Australia – British men over 21 living in Australia could vote
- 1902 women given right to vote and stand for parliament
- 1924 voting was made compulsory
- 1962 Aboriginal and Torres Strait Islander peoples gained right to vote
- 1973 voting age lowered from 21 to 18

IMAGINATIVE TEXT – Limerick

A limerick is a short, funny, rhyming poem with a singsong rhythm. Limericks have five lines and follow the same structure. The purpose of a limerick is to entertain and amuse.

3 Write a limerick about one of these characters.

a Who will your limerick be about? ______________________

b What makes your character unique? Write the first line.

____

c Write words that rhyme with the last word on the first line.

____

d What will happen to your character?

____

e Write your limerick.

____
____
____
____
____

PERSUASIVE TEXT – Movie review

A movie review is written to summarise and analyse a movie. It provides the audience with background information, a summary of the plot and descriptions of the characters.

4 Make notes to plan your review.

Movie title: ______________________

Director: ______________________

Year of release: ______________________

Characters: ______________________

Setting (place and time): ______________________

a Main events: ______________________

____

b Themes: ______________________

c Recommendation: ______________________

Write your movie review.

____
____
____
____
____
____

ANSWERS

Answers are not provided where students are asked to write their own texts.

TERM ONE

Unit 1

Page 2

1 **a** Q **b** C **c** C **d** E **e** S

2 Answers will vary.

Page 3

3 **a** Forgive your enemies. feeling
b Who is whispering behind the door? saying
c The car was going too fast along the road. doing
d Suddenly, Matt realised his mistake. thinking
e The class will have an excursion to the zoo next week. having

4 **a** P I rode my bike to school.
b N Australia is a federation of six states.
c F We will keep working until the end of term.
d N It has been raining for more than two weeks.
e P They had been building the house until the rain started.

5 Answers will vary.

Unit 2

Page 5

1-4 What is Static Electricity?

Static electricity is a build-up of charge on the surface of an object. It doesn't flow like current electricity.

All objects consist of atoms. Atoms consist of smaller particles: negatively charged electrons, positively charged protons and neutral neutrons. Mostly, the protons and electrons are balanced, and objects have no charge.

When surfaces of objects rub, electrons from one may move to the other. One becomes negatively charged and the other positively charged. Differently charged atoms attract, while atoms with a similar charge repel.

When you rub a balloon against your hair, the balloon takes electrons from your hair and becomes negatively charged. Your hair, now positively charged, tries to stick to the balloon. Conversely, each hair repels the others and sticks out wildly.

You may also have experienced static electricity if you were 'zapped' by a door handle, or even by shaking hands with a friend. Perhaps the biggest, hottest, loudest effect of static electricity you will experience is lightning. You see, static electricity surrounds us, but we don't always notice it.

3 Answers will vary. Examples:
a Most objects have no charge.
b Objects that are negatively charged attract objects that are positively charged and vice versa.
c When hair is positively charged, it tries to stick to the balloon which is negatively charged.
d Static electricity is all around us.

5 **a** negatively charged electrons
b positively charged protons
c differently charged atoms
d hair, now positively charged

6 **a** B Static electricity is a build-up of charge on the surface of an object.
b B Mostly, the protons and electrons are balanced.
c D Differently charged atoms attract.
d D Your hair tries to stick to the balloon.

7 **a** You may also have experienced static electricity if you were 'zapped' by a door handle.
b Perhaps the biggest, hottest, loudest effect of static electricity you will experience is lightning.

Unit 3

Page 6

1 Answers will vary. Example: What Causes Lightning?

2-5 Answers will vary.

Unit 4

Page 9

1, 2, 4 a, 5

Forbidden Fruit

My father bought several dwarf pear trees which he planted in the yard around the house. He watered them and fed them and watched them grow for many years. When at last one of the trees produced just one pear, he warned us that, under no circumstances, were we to pull that pear off the tree. "Whoever pulls that pear off the tree will be grounded for life," he said.

Every day, the pear grew larger, riper and more lusciously tempting. The sight of it made our mouths water – especially as we were forbidden to pull it off!

However, one of his children (I won't say who), carefully reasoned that it was not forbidden to touch the pear, nor even to eat it, only that it must not be "pulled off". That child bent down the limb that bore the pear, ate the juicy fruit, and left the core hanging on the tree!

3 Answers will vary. Example: Dad told the children that they weren't allowed to pull the pear off the tree, but it looked delicious and was hard to resist.

4 **b** The conclusion is funny because the child didn't pull the pear off the tree, but he ate it anyway.

6 Answers may vary. Example: My father only said that we weren't to pull the pear off the tree. He didn't say we couldn't touch it, or even eat it. So, I pulled down the branch and ate the pear right from the tree. I just left the core hanging there. I didn't pull it off the tree. It was very juicy too.

7 Answers may vary. Example: My father said, "Which one of you wicked children ate my precious pear?"
We all said, "It wasn't me."

Unit 6

Page 13

1, 2, 4–7, 9 a

The Tenterfield Oration by Sir Henry Parkes

(1889, an extract)

The great question which we have to consider is, whether the time has not now arisen for the creation on this Australian continent of an Australian government and an Australian parliament.

To make myself as plain as possible, Australia has now a population of three and a half million, and the American people numbered only between three and four million when they formed the great Commonwealth of the United States. The numbers are about the same. Surely what the Americans have done by war, Australians can bring about in peace.

Believing, as I do, that it is essential to preserve the security and integrity of these colonies, then the whole of our forces should be amalgamated into one great Federal army.

Seeing no other means of obtaining these ends, it seems to me that the time is close at hand when we ought to set about creating this great national Government for all Australia.

3 Answers will vary. Example: It is time for Australia to have one government and one parliament for all of Australia.

8 the great question we have to consider, to make myself as plain as possible, believing as I do, it seems to me

9 **b** great, have to, surely, peace, essential, preserve, security, integrity, should, ought, great

10 Answers may vary. Example: Henry Parkes was urging the people of Australia to form one Federal government for the whole of the country.

Term 1 Review

Page 18

1 Answers will vary. Examples:
a (Q) What happens when you rub a balloon against your hair?
b (C) Rub a balloon against your hair.
c (E) Your hair is sticking to the balloon!

2 Answers will vary. Examples:
a (Q) Why were the children forbidden to pick the only pear on the tree?
b (C) Do not pick the only pear on the tree.
c (E) Don't pick the pear!

3 a N I know all about static electricity. thinking
b P Henry Parkes delivered the Tenterfield Oration in 1889. saying
c P A huge crowd queued at the doughnut bakery. doing
d F It will be a very wet summer. being

4 Answers will vary.

Page 19

5-7 Answers will vary.

TERM TWO

Unit 9

Page 20

1 a Alex likes to read science fiction stories, but she doesn't like fantasy.
b The baker sold a lot of doughnuts, yet she made very little profit.
c The boy was upset, for someone had stolen his tablet.
d The people voted in a referendum, and they decided to remain a monarchy.

2 a The children weren't allowed to go to the beach, nor could they go to the movies.
b Static electricity isn't usually dangerous, nor will it hurt you.
c Doughnuts are not expensive, nor are they healthy food.

3 a so c for e and g or
b nor d but/yet f but/yet

Page 21

4 a S Doughnuts are delicious, but they are not good for you.
b F Tenterfield Oration 1889
c F north of Australia
d F free-range eggs
e S Hens can go outside during the day.
f S Fishing is a popular sport, and fish is a popular food.

5 An adaptation is anything that helps an organism survive in its environment. The environment in which an organism usually lives is called its habitat. The white fur of a polar bear is an adaptation to its environment, the icy Arctic. Polar bears have black skin underneath their fur, just like the brown bears they are descended from. White fur helps camouflage polar bears while they are hunting.

6 Answers will vary.

Unit 10

Page 23

1, 2, 4, 8

Country:	PAPUA NEW GUINEA
Location:	Oceania, eastern half of the island of New Guinea and offshore islands, north of Australia
Climate:	tropical
Population:	approx. 9 million
Capital:	Port Moresby
Language:	English, Hiri Motu, PNG Sign Language, Tok Pisin and 850 Indigenous languages
Currency:	Kina (PGK)
Environment:	mostly mountainous, covered with tropical rainforest
Trade:	minerals, such as gold, oil and copper, palm oil, coffee, cocoa and coconut oil
History:	The first people to live in Papua New Guinea arrived about 45,000 years ago. Until the 1800s, people lived in traditional communities. Many still do. From 1884 until 1975, Papua New Guinea was ruled by three external powers. Germany ruled the northern half of the country, called Guinea, while Britain ruled the southern part, called Papua. During World War I, Australia took over its administration. The two territories combined after World War II. In 1975, they became an independent country, called Papua New Guinea.

3 History

5 Answers will vary. Examples:
a Papua New Guinea has a tropical climate.
b Approximately 9 million people live in Papua New Guinea.
c Papua New Guinea is mostly tropical rainforest-covered mountains.

6

45,000 years ago	first people arrived
Until 1800s	people lived in traditional communities
1884–1975	ruled by 3 external powers
World War I	Australia took over administration
After WWII	territories combined
1975	became an independent country

7 Australia, Indonesia and the Solomon Islands

8 PNG = Papua New Guinea, PNK = Papua New Guinea Kina

Unit 12

Page 27

1, 2, 4 a

A Moment of Accidental Stupidity

It was spur-of-the-moment stupidity, an accident. One minute Oz was standing on the side of the road. The next minute he was huddling behind a silver crate in a spaceship.

Stamped on the crate was a picture of a constellation. It had an arrow pointing to one star. This struck Oz as an ingenious way to write an address. He just wished he knew where, exactly, that address was.

*Just before the moment of accidental stupidity, Oz had been standing behind a tree when a noise like a thousand five-year-olds having lollipops plucked from their fat, little lips sounded. The dusty verge at the side of the road puffed up in a willy-willy and sailed up the road despite there being no wind. The neighbour's goat bleated a warning and galloped away, dragging its chinking chain. In the tall grass in front of Oz appeared a gigantic silver ball with an open hatch. A small hovering robot zipped out of the hatch, up over the tree where Oz stood and off across the paddock.

3 Answers will vary. Example: Oz was abducted into a spaceship.

4 b Just before the moment of accidental stupidity.

5 Answers may vary. Examples: Where did this spaceship come from? Why is the spaceship here? What is the robot doing? Are they friendly?

6 a abducted into a spaceship
b a constellation for an address
c a robot coming out of a spaceship

7 a Oz was watching a robot zip across the paddock.
b The neighbour's goat was bleating a warning and galloping away.

Unit 14

Page 31

1, 2, 3 a, 3 b, 4 a, 5 a, 6 a

Should Fish be Farmed?

Since overfishing of our oceans has caused a decline in the numbers of fish, fish farming has become more important.

Fish farms produce fish much quicker than they reproduce in the wild. Currently, about one in four fish eaten by humans has been farmed. The World Bank estimates it will increase to two-thirds by 2030. China already gets about 80% of its fish from fish farms.

Fish farms help support poorer communities by employing more people and providing a cheap source of food.

However, farmed fish eat food made from other fish. This also leads to overfishing.

Fish farms pollute by increasing algae in oceans, which reduces the amount of oxygen available for other creatures.

Keeping large numbers of animals in confined spaces can lead to disease. Antibiotics and pesticides used to combat disease can harm marine and human health. If diseased fish escape, they can infect others in the wild.

Fish farming helps feed the world. However, fish farms must be managed efficiently.

ANSWERS

3 c For fish farming – increases production of fish – supports poorer communities

d Against fish farming – feeding fish instead of people – causes pollution – spreads disease

4 b Fish farms are beneficial when they are managed properly.

5 b more important, much quicker, help support, more, cheap, overfishing, pollute, reduces, disease, harm, infect, must

6 b has caused, has become, has been farmed

Term 2 Review

Page 36

1 a and b nor c but/yet d or e so f but/yet g for

2 a F 45,000 years ago

b S Many people in Papua New Guinea live in traditional communities.

c F New Zealand, Fiji, Indonesia

d F fish farming in marine environments

e S Freshwater fish farming is cheap and efficient.

f S Hens live in cages and are fed by machines.

3 Answers will vary

Page 37

4 & 5 Answers will vary

TERM THREE

Unit 17

Page 38

1 a Many people choose free-range eggs because the hens can go outside during the day.

b The farmers leave the shed doors open so (that) the hens can go outside.

c Since they are cheaper and the same nutritionally, many people choose cage eggs.

d Shoppers compare the prices of goods as they want the best value for money.

e Supermarkets position chocolate near the checkout so (that) customers will buy it.

Page 39

2 a Unless it stops raining soon, the river will flood.

b Although they were prepared for the storm season, they didn't expect so much hail.

c The children always take an umbrella if it looks like rain.

d The family spends every day on the beach unless it is raining.

3 a The children played outside after the storm had blown over.

b The cook checked the use-by date before she cracked the eggs.

c Oz was hiding in the spaceship when the robot returned.

d Whenever I think of fish farming, I think of riding seahorses.

4 Answers will vary. Examples:

a Fish farming is good *because* fish are produced quickly.

b I like to watch science fiction movies *whenever* a new one is released.

c I always brush my teeth *after* I have breakfast.

d I haven't been to the beach *where* the big rocks jut out into the ocean.

e I will not buy the eggs *if* any of them are damaged.

f Australia has had a national government *since* federation began in 1901.

g The children stayed inside *whenever* there was a storm raging outside.

h The robot came out of the spaceship *while* it was hovering above the trees.

i Papua New Guinea was ruled by other countries *before* it got independence.

j The baker didn't make money from doughnuts *as* nobody bought them.

Unit 18

Page 41

1, 2, 3 a, 4 a, 5 a

How to Inflate a Balloon Without Blowing

You may already be familiar with the way bicarb soda fizzes when vinegar is added. Now you can use that fizz to inflate a balloon.

Things you need

- bicarb soda
- vinegar
- a small plastic water bottle (make sure the neck is small enough for a balloon to fit on tightly)
- a funnel
- a balloon
- a teaspoon

Steps

1. Stretch the balloon a few times to make it softer and easier to inflate.
2. Pour vinegar into the bottle to half fill it.
3. Use a funnel to put 2 teaspoons of bicarb soda in the balloon.
4. Stretch the mouth of the balloon over the neck of the bottle so the bicarb soda falls into the vinegar.

As the gas, carbon dioxide, in the mixture rises, it will blow up the balloon.

3 b Things you need, Steps

4 b Stretch, Pour, Use, Stretch

5 b into, in, over, of, into

6 Answers will vary. Examples:

a Draw a picture on the cover of your book.

b Turn left at the next corner.

c Hold the balloon next to your hair.

d Put your plate in the dishwasher.

Unit 20

Page 45

1, 2, 4, 6, 7 a

High Explosive

by A. B. Banjo Paterson

'Twas the dingo pup to his dam that said,
"It's time I worked for my daily bread.
Out in the world I intend to go,
And you'd be surprised at the things I know.

"There's a wild duck's nest in a sheltered spot,
And I'll go right down and I'll eat the lot."
But when he got to his destined prey
He found that the ducks had flown away.

But an egg was left that would quench his thirst,
So he bit the egg and it straightway burst.
It burst with a bang, and he turned and fled,
For he thought that the egg had shot him dead.

"Oh, mother," he said, "let us clear right out
Or we'll lose our lives with the bombs about;
And it's lucky I am that I'm not blown up,
It's a very hard life," said the dingo pup.

3 a a dingo pup

b when the pup was old enough to go out on his own

c near a wild duck's nest in outback Australia

4 a The dingo pup was going to eat all the ducks in the nest.

b The dingo pup couldn't eat the ducks because they'd flown away.

c There was one egg left in the nest, so he decided to eat it instead.

d The egg burst and frightened the pup so much that he told his mother they should go somewhere else to live.

5 The dingo pup thought he'd been shot, but it was just a rotten egg that had burst.

7 b I'll = I will, we'll = we will, I'm = I am

ANSWERS

Unit 22

Page 49

1, 2 a, 3 a, 5 a

2 b Oswald is the best. He is the funniest. He sent critics home chortling. He gives people the loudest laughs. He's the cartoon sensation of the year.

3 b Universal Shorts are Super Shorts!

4 a I sent the critics home chortling with glee.
  b I gave the Criterion its loudest laffs in months.
  c I'm the cartoon sensation of the year.

5 b Krazy = crazy, Kartoon = cartoon, laffs = laughs, krazier = crazier, krazy kat = crazy cat

6 Answers will vary. Examples:
  a chortling, gelt, simoleons
  c chortling means laughing, gelt means money, simoleons means dollars

Term 3 Review

Page 54

1 a We stretch the balloon over the bottle so (that) the bicarb soda falls into the water.
  b The dingo pup left home because he wanted to find his own food.
  c If you like funny cartoons, you will love Oswald the Lucky Rabbit.
  d You might see a bandicoot when you are walking in the bush at night.
  e Although it was expensive, people queued for hours to buy the latest watch.

2 Answers will vary. Examples:
  a The children closed the windows *as the rain was coming in.*
  b The spectators cheered *after the sweeper kicked the goal.*
  c It will not be possible to go to the beach *unless it stops raining.*
  d His little sister followed him *wherever he went.*
  e I left home *before the sun was up.*
  f You may not have another apple *since there are no apples left.*

3 Answers will vary.

Page 55

4 & 5 Answers will vary.

TERM FOUR

Unit 25

Page 56

1 a Sir Henry Parkes, who was an Australian politician, delivered the Tenterfield Oration.
  b Oz was surprised by the spaceship that landed nearby.
  c The fisherman gave some fish to the children whom he met on the jetty.
  d Papua New Guinea, which lies to the north of Australia, is Australia's nearest neighbour.

2 Answers will vary. Examples:
  a The hen, that we got from the farmer next door, laid an egg every day.
  b The movie, that we saw last week, was the best this year.
  c The student, who won the science competition, made a fountain using bicarb soda and vinegar.
  d The family moved into a new house, which has a huge swimming pool.

Page 57

3 a Although free-range eggs are often more expensive, many people buy them.
  b I go fishing with my father whenever he takes the boat out.
  c The girl rubbed her hair with a balloon so that it would stick out all over.
  d After the storm had past, they saw a brilliant double rainbow.

4 a The wild duck's nest, which was hidden in a sheltered spot, was empty because the ducks had flown away.
  b Static electricity, which is a build-up of charge on the surface of an object, is not like current electricity which flows through a circuit.
  c You may have experienced static electricity if you were zapped by a door handle after you crossed a carpeted floor.
  d A constellation, that had an arrow pointing to a star, was stamped on the crate.

5 **Adaptation to climate change**

[Adaptation is possible.] [Some types of coral on the Great Barrier Reef have adapted to warmer water temperatures.] Coral need algae to survive, but warm water and intense sunlight kill the algae. Well-adapted corals produce a sunscreen-like substance that shields algae from the heat. Corals without this adaptation are likely to die off as seas get warmer.

Unit 26

Page 59

1–4, 6, 7 a

Australia Becomes a Federation

Before Federation, Australia did not have one unified government. Each colony had its own government.

Although the idea of a government for all Australia was suggested by Sir Henry Parkes in 1867, progress was slow until 1889. In that year, two events helped move Australia towards Federation. The first was a report by Major-General J. Bevan Edwards who suggested that Australia needed a national army to protect itself. Sir Henry Parkes reiterated the need in his famous speech at Tenterfield later that year. From 1890, delegates from the colonies met to draft a constitution. When the draft was complete, referendums were held in 1898 and 1899 to gain approval from the people. After that, it was necessary for the British Government and Monarch to also agree.

On 17 September 1900, Queen Victoria proclaimed that the Commonwealth of Australia would become a Federation on 1 January 1901.

ANSWERS

3 Answers may vary, but will include the following items:
  a 1867 Sir Henry Parkes suggested government for all Australia
  b 1889 Major-General J. Bevan Edwards said national army was needed
  c 1889 Sir Henry Parkes Tenterfield speech
  d 1890 constitution was drafted
  e 1898 and 1899 referendums for approval
  f 1900 Queen Victoria proclaimed Commonwealth of Australia
  g 1 January 1901 Australia became a Federation

5 Answers may vary. Examples: the idea of a government for all Australia, a report by Major-General J. Bevan Edwards, a national army to protect itself, delegates from the colonies

7 b before, in, until, later, from, after, on

Unit 28

Page 63

1, 2, 5, 6

Three Limericks by Edward Lear

There was an Old Man with a Beard

There was an Old Man with a beard,
Who said, "It is just as I feared! –
Two Owls and a Hen,
Four Larks and a Wren,
Have all built their nests in my beard."

There was an Old Man in a Tree

There was an Old Man in a tree,
Who was horribly bored by a Bee;
When they said, "Does it buzz?"
He replied, "Yes, it does!
It's a regular brute of a Bee!"

There was an Old Man in a Barge

There was an Old Man in a barge,
Whose nose was exceedingly large;
But in fishing by night,
It supported a light,
Which helped that Old Man in a barge.

3 Answers will vary. Examples:
  Limerick 1: Birds built their nests in the Old Man's beard.
  Limerick 2: The Old Man got stung by a bee.
  Limerick 3: The Old Man hung a light from his nose so he could see to fish at night.

4 Answers will vary. Examples:
  Limerick 1: Birds don't usually build nests in beards.
  Limerick 2: The Old Man said the Bee was a brute. Brutes are usually big.
  Limerick 3: People's noses aren't usually long enough to hang lights from them.

Unit 30

Page 67

1–4 a, 5, 6, 10

Rabbit-Proof Fence

Director: Phillip Noyce
Released: February 2002
Based on a true story.
The movie, which is set in Western Australia in 1931, is about three Aboriginal girls. The girls are stolen from their mothers and taken to live in a settlement over two thousand kilometres away.
The girls are treated harshly at the settlement, forced to forget their culture, and not permitted to speak their own language. They escape and make an arduous journey home, following the rabbit-proof fence.
About family, love and belonging, the movie is highly emotive. We cannot help but feel pain at the injustice the girls experience. We also fear for their safety on their epic journey. However, we must also admire their determination, resourcefulness and resilience.
I recommend this movie for adults and children over 11 years who enjoy adventure stories, and especially those who wish to gain a better understanding of Australia's history.

3 Where: Western Australia
  When: 1931
  Who: three Aboriginal girls who were stolen from their mothers

4 b The girls are stolen from their mothers; they are treated harshly at the settlement; they escape, and they journey home.

7 adults and children over 11 years who enjoy adventure stories

8 Aboriginal and Torres Strait Islander peoples

9 Answers may vary. Examples: their mothers, a settlement over two thousand kilometres away, the settlement, their culture, their own language, their epic journey, this movie

Unit 32

Page 70

1 Movie title: Storm Boy
  Director: Shawn Seet
  Year of release: 2019
  Characters: Mike, three orphaned pelicans, Fingerbone, Mr Percival
  Setting (place and time): isolated beach in South Australia, modern setting

2 Answers will vary. Examples: friendship, caring for animals, the environment

3 Answers will vary. Examples: not scary, sentimental, sad, disappointing, heartwarming

4 Answers will vary. Example: I recommend this movie for viewers over 8 years who enjoy movies about animals.

Term 4 Review

Page 72

1 a Queen Victoria, who was the ruling monarch, proclaimed Australia a Federation because the people had voted in favour of it.

b Since Australia became a Federation in 1901, there have been 19 referendums which have led to eight changes to the constitution.

c In the first referendum, which was held in 1906, the people agreed that both houses of parliament could be elected at the same time.

d A limerick is a short, funny, rhyming poem that is written to entertain and amuse.

e The old man, who had a big, bushy beard, went to the barber because animals started to nest in it.

f The movie, which is about three Aboriginal girls who were stolen from their mothers, is called Rabbit-Proof Fence.

g The girls, who escaped from the settlement, followed the rabbit-proof fence until they were reunited with their mothers.

h The movie, Storm Boy, is not recommended for really young children because they may be sad when the hunters shoot the pelicans.

2 Answers will vary.

Page 73

3 & 4 Answers will vary.

Targeting Writing Skills Year 6

ISBN: 9781925726299
Published by Pascal Press
PO Box 250
Glebe NSW 2037
www.pascalpress.com.au
contact@pascalpress.com.au
Design: Janice Bowles
Author: Norah Colvin
Publisher: Lynn Dickinson
Editor: Marie Theodore
Typesetter: Stacey Grainger
Illustrator: Paul Lennon

Printed by Wai Man Book Binding (China) Ltd.